SAMUEL L. BRENGLE

THE SERVANT'S HEART

Bob Hostetler, General Editor

wesleyan
PUBLISHING HOUSE
wphstore.com

CREST BOOKS

Copyright © 2016 by The Salvation Army
Published by Wesleyan Publishing House
Indianapolis, Indiana 46250
Printed in the United States of America
ISBN: 978-1-63257-068-0
ISBN (e-book): 978-1-63257-069-7

Library of Congress Cataloging-in-Publication Data

Brengle, Samuel Logan, 1860-1936.
   The servant's heart / Samuel L. Brengle ; Bob Hostetler, general editor.
      pages cm. -- (Samuel L. Brengle's holy life series)
   ISBN 978-1-63257-068-0 (pbk.)
   1. Witness bearing (Christianity) 2. Evangelistic work. 3. Christian life. I. Hostetler,
Bob, 1958- editor. II. Title.
   BV4520.B645 2016
   248'.5--dc23
                                    2015026516

This work is a revised combination of the following book from The Salvation Army:
The Soul-Winner's Secret and *Love Slaves*.

Contents

Preface

Samuel Logan Brengle was an influential author, teacher, and preacher on the doctrine of holiness in the late nineteenth to early twentieth century, serving from 1887–1931 as an active officer (minister) in The Salvation Army. In 1889 while he and his wife, Elizabeth Swift Brengle, were serving as corps officers (pastors) in Boston, Massachusetts, a brick thrown by a street "tough" smashed Brengle's head against a door frame and caused an injury severe enough to require more than nineteen months of convalescence. During that treatment and recuperation period, he began writing articles on holiness for The Salvation Army's publication, *The War Cry*, which were later collected and published as a "little red book" under the title *Helps to Holiness*. That book's success led to eight others over the next forty-five years: *Heart Talks on Holiness*, *The Way of Holiness*, *The Soul-Winner's Secret*, *When the Holy Ghost Is Come*, *Love-Slaves*, *Resurrection Life and Power*,

Ancient Prophets and Modern Problems, and *The Guest of the Soul* (published in his retirement in 1934).

By the time of his death in 1936, Commissioner Brengle was an internationally renowned preacher and worldwide ambassador of holiness. His influence continues today, perhaps more than any Salvationist in history besides the founders, William and Catherine Booth.

I hope that the revised and updated editions of his books that comprise the Samuel L. Brengle's Holy Life Series will enhance and enlarge that influence, introduce these writings to new readers, and create fresh interest in those who already know the godly wisdom and life-changing power of these volumes.

While I have taken care to preserve the integrity, impact, and voice of the original writing, I have carefully and prayerfully made changes that I hope will facilitate greater understanding and appreciation of Brengle's words for modern readers. These changes include:

- Revising archaic terms (such as the use of King James English) and updating the language to reflect more contemporary usage (such as occasionally employing more inclusive gender references);
- Shortening and simplifying sentence structure and revising punctuation to conform more closely to contemporary practice;
- Explaining specific references of The Salvation Army that will not be familiar to the general population;
- Updating Scripture references (when possible retaining the King James Version—used exclusively in Brengle's writings—but frequently incorporating modern versions, especially when doing so will aid the reader's comprehension and enjoyment);

- Replacing Roman numerals with Arabic numerals and spelled out Scripture references for the sake of those who are less familiar with the Bible;

- Citing Scripture quotes not referenced in the original and noting the sources for quotes, lines from hymns, etc.;

- Aligning all quoted material to the source (Brengle, who often quoted not only Scripture, but also poetry from memory, often quoted loosely in speaking and writing);

- Adding occasional explanatory phrases or endnotes to identify people or events that might not be familiar to modern readers;

- Revising or replacing some chapter titles, and (in *Ancient Prophets and Modern Problems*) moving one chapter to later in the book; and

- Deleting the prefaces that introduced each book and epigraphs that preceded some chapters.

In the preface to Brengle's first book, Commissioner (later General) Bramwell Booth wrote, "This book is intended to help every reader of its pages into the immediate enjoyment of Bible holiness. Its writer is an officer of The Salvation Army who, having a gracious experience of the things whereof he writes, has been signally used of God, both in life and testimony, to the sanctifying of the Lord's people, as well as in the salvation of sinners. I commend him and what he has here written down to every lover of God and His kingdom here on earth."

In the preface to Brengle's last book, *The Guest of the Soul*, The Salvation Army's third general (and successor to Bramwell Booth) wrote: "These choice contributions . . . will, I am sure, serve to strengthen the faith of the readers of this book and impress upon them the joyousness of life when the heart has been opened to the Holy Guest of the Soul."

I hope and pray that this updated version of Brengle's writings will further those aims.

—Bob Hostetler

general editor

PART ONE

The Soul-Winner's Secret

The Personal Experience of the Soul-Winner **1**

Every soul-winner is in the secret of the Lord and has had a definite personal experience of salvation and the baptism of the Holy Spirit, which brings him or her into close fellowship, tender friendship, and sympathy with the Savior. The psalmist prayed, "Purify me from my sins. . . . Remove the stain of my guilt. Create in me a clean heart, O God. Renew a loyal spirit within me. Do not banish me from your presence, and don't take your Holy Spirit from me. Restore to me the joy of your salvation, and make me willing to obey you" (Ps. 51:7, 9–12 NLT).

"Then," said he, "I will teach your ways to rebels, and they will return to you" (Ps. 51:13 NLT). He saw that before he could be a soul-winner, before he could teach others the way of the Lord and lead them to salvation, he must have his own sins blotted out; he must have a clean heart and a right spirit, and he must be a partaker of the Holy Spirit and of God's joy. In short, he must have a definite, constant, joyful experience of God's salvation in his own soul in order to save others. It was no "hope I am saved" experience he wanted, nor was it a conclusion carefully reasoned out and arrived at by logical processes. It was not an experience based upon a strict performance of a set round of duties and attendance upon sacraments, but a mighty transformation and cleansing of his whole spiritual nature and a glorious new creation wrought within him by the Holy Spirit.

This must be a definite experience that tallies with the Word of God. Only this can give that power and assurance which will enable you to lead and win others. You must have knowledge before you can impart knowledge. You must have fire to kindle fire. You must have life to reproduce life. You must know Jesus and be on friendly terms with Him to be able to introduce others to Him. You must be one with Jesus and be "bound up in the bundle of life" (1 Sam. 25:29 KJV) with Him if you would bring others into that life.

Peter had repented under John the Baptist's preaching, had forsaken all to follow Jesus, had waited with prayer and unquenchable desire until he received the baptism of the Holy Spirit and of fire, and had been anointed with power from on high before he became the fearless, mighty preacher who won three thousand souls in a day.

Paul was mightily changed on the road to Damascus, heard Jesus' voice tell him what to do, and was baptized with the Holy Spirit under Ananias's teaching before he became the apostle of quenchless zeal who turned the world upside down.

Luther was definitely transformed and justified by faith on the stairway of St. Peter's in Rome before he became the invincible reformer who could stand before popes and emperors and set captive nations free.

George Fox, John Wesley, Charles Finney, George Whitefield, Jonathan Edwards, William Taylor, James Caughey, Dwight L. Moody, and William Booth all had definite personal experiences that made them apostles of fire, prophets of God, and winners of souls. They did not guess that they had experienced new life in Christ, nor "hope" so, but they knew in Whom they believed (see 2 Tim. 1:12) and knew that they had passed from darkness into light and from the power of Satan to God (see Acts 26:18).

This experience was not spiritual evolution but revolution. No evolutionist ever has been or ever will be a great soul-winner. It is not by growth that we become such, but by revelation. It is not until God bursts through the veil to reveal Himself in our hearts through faith in His dear Son; gives a consciousness of personal acceptance with Him; and sheds abroad His love in the heart, destroying unbelief, burning away sin, consuming selfishness, and filling the soul with the passion that filled the heart of Jesus, that we become soul-winners.

The experience that makes a man or woman a soul-winner is twofold. First, we must know our sins to be forgiven. We must have recognized ourselves to be sinners, out of friendly relations with God, careless of God's claim, heedless of God's feelings, selfishly seeking our own way in spite of divine love and compassion, and heedless of the awful consequences of separating ourselves from God. This must then have led to repentance toward God, by which I mean sorrow for and an utter turning away from sin, followed by a confiding trust in Jesus Christ as our Savior. We must have so believed as to bring a restful consciousness that for Christ's sake our sins have been forgiven and we have been adopted into God's family and made one of His dear children.

This consciousness results from what Paul called the witness of the Spirit (see Rom. 8:16) and enables the soul to cry out in deep filial confidence and affection, "Abba, Father" (Rom. 8:15 NLT).

Second, we must be sanctified. We must know that our heart is cleansed, that pride and self-will and carnal ambition and strife and sensitiveness and suspicion and unbelief and every unholy temper are destroyed by the baptism of the Holy Spirit. We must experience a personal Pentecost and the incoming of a great love for, and loyalty to, Jesus Christ.

It must be a constant experience. People who frequently meet defeat in their own souls will not be largely successful in winning others to Jesus. The very consciousness of defeat makes them uncertain in their exhortation, doubtful and wavering in their testimony, and weak in their faith. This will not be likely to produce conviction and beget faith in their hearers.

Finney, Wesley, Fletcher of Madeley, William Bramwell, Catherine Booth, and scores of others walked with God, as Enoch did, and so walked "in the power of the Spirit" (Luke 4:14 KJV) constantly and were soul-winners all their lives.

It must be a joyful experience. "The joy of the LORD is your strength," said Nehemiah (Neh. 8:10 KJV). "Restore to me the joy of your salvation," prayed David (Ps. 51:12 NLT).

"I feel it my duty to be as happy as the Lord wants me to be," wrote Robert Murray McCheyne, the gifted and deeply spiritual Scottish preacher, who was wonderfully successful in winning souls.

William Caughey, while preaching his sermon entitled "The Striving of the Spirit," cried out, "Oh, my soul is very happy! Bless God! I feel He is with me!"[1] No wonder he won souls.

Whitefield and Bramwell, two of the greatest soul-winners the world ever saw, were at times in almost an ecstasy of joy, especially when preaching. And this was as it should be.

John Bunyan told us how he wrote *The Pilgrim's Progress* in his filthy Bedford dungeon. He said, "So I was led home to prison, and I sat me down and wrote and wrote because joy did make me write."

God wants His people to be full of joy. Jesus said, "These things have I spoken unto you, that my joy might remain in you, and that your joy might be full" (John 15:11 KJV). And again He said, "Ask and you will receive, and your joy will be complete" (John 16:24 NIV). John wrote, "And these things we write to you that your joy may be full" (1 John 1:4 NKJV). "The fruit of the Spirit is . . . joy," wrote Paul (Gal. 5:22 KJV), and again he wrote, "The Kingdom of God is . . . living a life of goodness and peace and joy in the Holy Spirit" (Rom. 14:17 NLT). Joy in the Holy Spirit is an oceanic current that flows unbroken through the holy, believing soul, even when surrounded by seas of trouble and compassed about by infirmities and afflictions and sorrows.

We so often have thought of Jesus as the "man of sorrows" (Isa. 53:3 KJV) as to overlook His fullness of exultant joy.

Joy can and should be cultivated, just as faith or any other fruit of the Spirit is cultivated:

- By appropriating by faith the words that were spoken and written for the express purpose of giving us fullness of joy. "May the God of hope fill you with all joy and peace in believing" (Rom. 15:13 ESV), wrote Paul to the Romans. It is by believing.

- By meditating on these words and holding them in our minds and hearts as we would hold honey in our mouths, until we have gotten all the sweetness out of them.

- By exercise, even as faith or love or patience is exercised. This we do by rejoicing in the Lord and praising God for His goodness and mercy, and shouting when the joy wells up in our souls under the pressure of the Holy Spirit. Many people quench the spirit of joy and praise, and so gradually lose it. But let them repent, confess, pray, and believe, and then begin to praise God again, and He will see to it that they have something to praise Him for. Then their joy will convict others and prove a mighty means of winning souls to Jesus.

Who can estimate the power there must have been in the joy that filled the heart of Peter and surged through the souls and beamed on the faces and flashed from the eyes of the 120 fire-baptized disciples, while he preached that Pentecostal sermon which won three thousand bigoted enemies to the cross of a crucified Christ? O Lord, still "make [Thy] ministers a flame of fire" (Heb. 1:7 KJV) and flood the world with Your mighty joy!

NOTE

1. Brengle may have been mistaken in referencing Caughey's sermon, "The Striving of the Spirit." In a collection of Caughey's sermons containing that sermon, another sermon—"Purification by Faith"—contains the words, "My God is in this place; He is here; I feel Him blessing this poor little heart; my soul is very happy." (James Caughey, "Purification by Faith," *Helps to a Life of Holiness and Usefulness, or Revival Miscellanies* [Boston: J. P. Magee, 1852], 36.)

Obedience 2

"I was not disobedient to the vision from heaven," said Paul (Acts 26:19 NIV), and in that saying he revealed the secret of his wonderful success as a soul-winner. Soul-winners are men and women sent by God, who will receive direct orders that, if affectionately heeded and heartily and courageously obeyed, will surely lead to success. They are preeminently workers together with God (see 2 Cor. 6:1) and soldiers of Jesus Christ, and as such must obey. It is their business to take orders and carry them out.

The Lord said to Jeremiah, "I knew you before I formed you in your mother's womb. Before you were born I set you apart and appointed you as my prophet to the nations" (Jer. 1:5 NLT). And when Jeremiah interrupted and said, "O Sovereign LORD . . . I can't speak for you! I'm too young!" the Lord said to him, "Don't say, 'I'm too young,' for you must go wherever I send you and say whatever I tell you. And don't be afraid of the people, for I will be with you and will protect you. I, the LORD, have spoken! . . . Get up and prepare for action. Go out and tell them everything I tell you to say. Do not be afraid of them, or I will make you look foolish in front of them" (Jer. 1:6–8, 17 NLT).

Soul-winners must get their message from God and speak what and when He commands. They are servants of God, friends of Jesus, prophets of the Most High, ambassadors of heaven to the citizens of this world, and they must speak heaven's words and represent heaven's court and King and not seek their own will, but the will of Him who sent them. "To obey is better than sacrifice" (1 Sam. 15:22 KJV). They must not trim their course to suit others, nor stop to ask what this or that person would do, but must attend strictly to the Lord and steadfastly follow Jesus. Paul told us that Jesus was "obedient unto death" (Phil. 2:8 KJV), and again and again he called himself a servant of Jesus Christ.

This obedience must be prompt. In spite of the appeals and encouragements of Joshua and Caleb, the children of Israel refused to go over into Canaan. But afterward, seeing their sin in refusing to obey promptly, they attempted to go over in spite of the warnings of Moses not now to do so, and met with bitter defeat. Promptness would have saved them forty years of wandering in the wilderness.

Once the soul-winner knows the Master's will, there must be no delay to fulfill it. If you are in doubt, you can take time to assure yourself as to what that will is. God would not have you run before you are sure you are sent, nor go before you have a message, nor falter and possibly fall because of uncertainty. But once you have received your orders and your message, remember that "the king's business require[s] haste" (1 Sam. 21:8 KJV). Strike while the iron is hot. Act and speak when the Spirit moves, and do not dilly-dally like covetous Balaam to see if God will change His mind and His orders.

American admiral George Dewey's matchless victory at Manila (during the Spanish-American War) was won, and the geographical boundaries of the nations changed, by the promptness with which he carried out his orders to destroy the Spanish fleet. I have noticed that if I speak when the Spirit moves me, I can usually introduce the subject of religion and God's claims to any individual or group with happy results. But if I delay, the opportunity slips by, not to return again, or if it does return, it does so with increased difficulties.

This obedience must be exact. Saul lost his kingdom and his life because his obedience was only partial (see 1 Sam. 15). So also did the prophet who warned the wicked King Jeroboam (see 1 Kings 13).

By contrast, Mary told the servants at the marriage in Cana, "Do whatever he tells you" (John 2:5 NLT), and when they obeyed Him, Jesus performed His first miracle. And so He will work miracles today through His chosen people, if they will do whatever He says. Then they will find that it is not themselves but the Spirit who speaks in them, so that they can say with Jesus, "The words I speak are not my own, but my Father who lives in me does his work through me" (John 14:10 NLT). For did not Jesus say, "Ask for anything in my name, and I will do it" (John 14:13 NLT)?

This obedience must be courageous. "Don't be afraid of the people," said the Lord to Jeremiah (Jer. 1:8 NLT). And He said to Ezekiel, "Son of man, do not fear them or their words. Don't be afraid even though their threats surround you like nettles and briers and stinging scorpions. Do not be dismayed by their dark scowls, even though they are rebels. You must give them my messages whether they listen or not!" (Ezek. 2:6–7 NLT).

He was not to say that which would please the people, but that which God gave him to say, and that without fear of consequences, for God would be with him.

"Then Saul admitted to Samuel, 'Yes, I have sinned. I have disobeyed your instructions and the LORD's command, for I was afraid of the people and did what they demanded'" (1 Sam. 15:24 NLT). No wonder God cast him off and gave his crown and kingdom to another! God said, "Don't be afraid, for I am with you. Don't be discouraged, for I am your God. I will strengthen you and help you. I will hold you up with my victorious right hand" (Isa. 41:10 NLT).

Let all soul-winners recognize that they are on picket duty for heaven, and let them throw themselves on heaven's protection and rest in the assurance of their heavenly Father's care and in Jesus' utmost sympathy and support. Let them do their duty courageously, saying with Paul, "I can do everything through Christ, who gives me strength" (Phil. 4:13 NLT).

Again and again I have comforted myself with good King Jehoshaphat's assurance: "Deal courageously and the LORD shall be with the good" (2 Chron. 19:11 KJV). I have encouraged myself with Peter's bold declaration to the enraged and outwitted Sanhedrin: "We must obey God rather than any human authority" (Acts 5:29 NLT). And I have measured myself by Nehemiah's self-forgetful words: "Should someone in my position run from danger? Should someone in my position enter the Temple to save his life? No, I won't do it!" (Neh.

6:11 NLT). And Paul's: "My life is worth nothing to me unless I use it for finishing the work assigned me by the Lord Jesus—the work of telling others the Good News about the wonderful grace of God" (Acts 20:24 NLT). And the three Hebrew children's: "O Nebuchadnezzar, we do not need to defend ourselves before you. If we are thrown into the blazing furnace, the God whom we serve is able to save us. He will rescue us from your power, Your Majesty. But even if he doesn't, we want to make it clear to you, Your Majesty, that we will never serve your gods or worship the gold statue you have set up" (Dan. 3:16–18 NLT). That is the kind of stuff out of which God makes soul-winners.

Do you ask, how can a man or woman get such a spirit of courageous obedience? I answer, by dying—dying to your selfish interests, to the love of praise, to the fear of censure, and to the hope of reward in this world—by a daredevil faith in the reward that God will give in the world to come, by a steadfast looking unto and following of Jesus, and by a constant comparison of time with eternity. I read the other day that it was only dead men who were living preachers.

The obedience must be glad. The command is, "Serve the LORD with gladness" (Ps. 100:2 KJV). "I take joy in doing your will, my God," wrote the psalmist (Ps. 40:8 NLT). There was no grudging about his obedience; it was his joy. It is a love service God wants, and that is always a joy service. "My meat is to do the will of him that sent me," said Jesus (John 4:34 KJV), and Paul declared, "If I do this thing willingly, I have a reward" (1 Cor. 9:17 KJV). It is a glad love service God calls us to, and once we are wholly His and the Comforter abides in us, we shall not find it irksome to obey. And by obedience we shall both save ourselves and others to whom the Lord may send us.

Let me hear Thy voice now speaking,

Let me hear and I'll obey;

While before Thy cross I'm seeking,

O chase my fears away!

O let the light now falling

Reveal my every need,

Now hear me while I'm calling,

O speak, and I will heed!

Let me hear and I will follow

Though the path be strewed with thorns;

It is joy to share Thy sorrow,

Thou makest calm the storm.

Now my heart Thy temple making,

In Thy fullness dwell with me;

Every evil way forsaking,

Thine only I will be.[1]

NOTE

1. Herbert Booth, "Let Me Hear Thy Voice Now Speaking," *The Salvation Army Songbook*, 1913, public domain.

Prayer **3**

Prayer is the way of approach to God, and the soul-winner keeps it open by constant use. It is the channel by which all spiritual blessings and power are received, and therefore the life of the soul-winner must be one of ceaseless prayer. "Pray without ceasing," wrote Paul (1 Thess. 5:17 KJV). It is the breath of the soul, and other things being equal, it is the secret of power.

It was written of Jesus, "And it came to pass in those days, that he went out into a mountain to pray, and continued all night in prayer to God" (Luke 6:12 KJV). And this was followed by mighty works.

What an amazing statement is this: "Whatever you ask in prayer, believe that you have received it, and it will be yours" (Mark 11:24 ESV). And this: "If you abide in me, and my words abide in you, ask whatever you wish, and it will be done for you" (John 15:7 ESV). And yet, amazing as these promises are, they stand there in "the Book of Truth" (Dan. 10:21 NLT) as a challenge to every child of God who is passionate about God's glory, longs for the triumph of righteousness, and seeks the salvation of souls.

Soul-winners must pray in secret. They must get alone with God and pour their hearts into the Father's ear with intercessions and pleadings and arguments if they would have success. There is no substitute for much wide awake, expectant, secret waiting upon God for the outpouring of the Holy Spirit, the gift of wisdom, strength, courage, hope, faith, and discernment. If we fail at this point, we will soon fail at every point. Jesus said, "When you pray, go into your room and shut the door and pray to your Father who is in secret. And your Father who sees in secret will reward you" (Matt. 6:6 ESV).

Here, then, is one secret of success: communion and counselings and conversations in the closet with God, who is our Father, and who can and will no more turn away from us when we come in the spirit of an obedient and affectionate child than can the sunlight when we throw open the windows and doors and stand in its beams. I say it reverently. He cannot turn away from us but will surely reward us — and openly, because He said He would, and He cannot lie.

Prayer must be definite. Once, when Jesus was leaving Jericho, blind Bartimaeus sat by the wayside begging, and when he heard Jesus was passing by, he cried out, "Jesus, Son of David, have mercy on me." But that prayer was not definite—it was altogether too general. Jesus knew what Bartimaeus wanted, but He desired Bartimeus to state exactly what he desired, and said to him, "What do you want me to do for you?" Then the blind man prayed a definite prayer—"Rabbi, let me recover my sight"—and the definite prayer then received a definite answer, for Jesus said to him, "Go your way; your faith has made you well," and immediately he received his sight (Mark 10:46–52 ESV).

We should be as definite when we go to God, in asking Him for what we want, as we are when we go to the store. The salesman is prepared to sell us anything and everything in the store, but he in reality sells us nothing until we tell him what we want, and so it is with our heavenly Father.

Our prayers must be bold. Paul said, "Let us come boldly unto the throne of grace, that we may obtain mercy, and find grace to help in time of need" (Heb. 4:16 KJV). Of course, this boldness must be coupled with humility, but the greater the humility, the greater the boldness, if mixed with faith. I have often been amused and amazed at the boldness with which children come to their parents for the things they need and the things they want, and how gladly the loving parents respond to the child's request, especially if the child expresses a genuine need! And Jesus said: "If you, then, though you are evil, know how to give good gifts to your children, how much more will your Father in heaven give good gifts to those who ask him!" (Matt. 7:11 NIV).

The Devil stands mocking and teasing praying souls to drive them from their knees and from their Father's face, but let them rather come boldly in the name of Jesus and wait patiently for the things they desire, and they shall have an abundant reward. It is not our heavenly Father's will to disappoint His trusting children, but rather to give them their utmost desire, "exceeding abundantly" (Eph. 3:20 KJV) above all they ask or think, for His heart is all love toward them. Therefore let us not be timid and wavering, but steadfast and bold as His dear children.

Prayer must be persistent and persevering. Jesus taught this very clearly in His parable of the importunate friend:

> Suppose you went to a friend's house at midnight, wanting to borrow three loaves of bread. You say to him, "A friend of mine has just arrived for a visit, and I have nothing for him to eat." And suppose he calls out from his bedroom, "Don't bother me. The door is locked for the night, and my family and I are all in bed. I can't help you." But I tell you this—though he won't do it for friendship's sake, if you keep knocking long enough, he will get up and give you whatever you need because of your shameless persistence. (Luke 11:5–8 NLT)

Then Jesus added, "Keep on asking, and you will receive what you ask for. Keep on seeking, and you will find. Keep on knocking, and the door will be opened to you" (Luke 11:9 NLT). With those words, Jesus meant to teach that we are to hold on in prayer till we get an answer. If the answer is delayed, our own hearts will be searched, the purity of our motives will be proven, and our faith will be purified, tried, developed, and strengthened for future and greater triumph.

Jesus prayed three times that the cup of death in the garden of Gethsemane might pass from Him. It was not death on the cross but death in the garden He feared. And the writer of Hebrews told us that He was heard (see Heb. 5:7). Daniel abstained from all pleasant food for three weeks at one time, and prayed until God appeared to him and said, "Don't be afraid . . . for you are very precious to God. Peace! Be encouraged! Be strong!" (Dan. 10:19 NLT), and added, "I will tell you what is written in the Book of Truth" and then told him all he desired to know (Dan. 10:21 NLT). And Elijah, after his victory over the priests of Baal, sent his servant seven times to look for the cloud that would bring rain, while he bowed his face between his knees and poured out his heart to God in prayer until the cloud appeared. Though the answer may be delayed, it is not God's purpose to deny us without letting us know the reason why.

Prayer must be for the glory of God and according to His will. If we ask things simply to gratify our own desires, God cannot grant them. James said of some, "You ask and do not receive, because you ask wrongly, to spend it on your passions" (James 4:3 ESV). But John said, "This is the confidence that we have toward him, that if we ask anything according to his will he hears us. And if we know that he hears us in whatever we ask, we know that we have the requests that we have asked of him" (1 John 5:14–15 ESV). Jesus said, "If you abide in me, and my words abide in you, ask whatever you wish, and it will be done for you" (John 15:7 ESV).

We are to ask according to the things revealed as His will in His Word and according to the principles laid down in it. Therefore we should study His Word constantly and hide it in our own hearts, and see to it that we hide ourselves in His heart and thus be filled with the truth. We shall then not ask amiss and, being filled with the Spirit, we shall not be denied.

Prayer must be mixed with faith. It must be believing prayer. "Whatever you ask in prayer, believe that you have received it, and it will be yours" (Mark 11:24 ESV). Oh, what a victory I got one morning over the Devil, when he tried to shake my faith and confidence! I laid hold of that promise and wrestled through to the solid rock of believing prayer, and had one of the most glorious soul-saving days in my life! The person whose faith is constantly wavering shall receive nothing from the Lord (see James 1:6–7).

Finally, prayer must be in the name of Jesus. "Whatever you ask in my name, this I will do, that the Father may be glorified in the Son," said Jesus (John 14:13 ESV). "The blood, the blood is all my plea,"[1] and with that plea the vilest sinner may come, while those born of God may approach with unabashed boldness into the presence of their heavenly Father and claim all the resources of heaven in their warfare against sin and in their effort to win souls and build up the kingdom of God.

NOTE

1. F. C. Baker "I Knew That God in His Word Had Spoken," 1885, public domain.

Zeal 4

It is said that Civil War general Philip Sheridan went to battle with all the fury of a madman. He claimed he never went into a battle from which he cared to come back alive unless he returned as a victor. This desperation made him an irresistible inspiration to his own troops and enabled him to hurl them like thunderbolts against his foes. If he became so desperate in killing people, how much more desperate, if possible, should we become in our effort and desire to see them enter into new life!

It was written of Jesus, "Zeal for your house will consume me" (John 2:17 ESV), and so it can be of every great soul-winner.

Not until a person can say with Paul, "My life is worth nothing to me unless I use it for finishing . . . the work of telling others the Good News about the wonderful grace of God" and "I am ready . . . to die . . . for the sake of the Lord Jesus" (Acts 20:24; 21:13 NLT) can he or she hope to be largely used in winning souls. Those who are anxious about their dinner, eager to get to bed at a reasonable hour, concerned about their salary, querulous about their reputation, and afraid of weariness and pain and headache and heartache will not make great soul-winners.

There are various kinds of zeal that should be avoided as deadly evils.

1. Partial zeal, like that of Jehu (see 2 Kings 10:15–31). God set him to destroy the wicked house of Ahab and the worship of Baal, and he did so with fury. "But Jehu did not obey the Law of the LORD, the God of Israel, with all his heart. He refused to turn from the sins that Jeroboam had led Israel to commit" (2 Kings 10:31 NLT). And in due time God had to cut off his dynasty as well.

This kind of zeal is frequently seen in those who violently attack one sort of sin while they themselves secretly indulge in some other sin. Such people are usually not only intolerant of the sin, but also of the sinner, while true zeal makes one infinitely tender and patient toward the sinner, while absolutely uncompromising with the sin.

2. Party zeal like that of the Pharisees and Sadducees. In these days, it takes the form of excessive sectarian and denominational zeal, and makes bigots of people. Zeal for the particular church or organization to which one belongs is right within certain limits. We come to faith through the instrumentality of a certain religious organization and we become children of its household, or we are led into it by the Holy Spirit through a blessed, divine affinity with its members, methods, spirit, and doctrine. In that case, we should be loyal and true to its leaders who are over us in the Lord and who watch for our souls, and follow them as they follow Christ.

We should also be loyal to the principles of the organization so far as they harmonize with the Word of God, and we should by prayer and supplication and ceaselessly zealous work seek to build up this organization in holiness and righteousness. And this we can do with all our might, if we do it in the Holy Spirit, and can be assured that God is well pleased with us. But we must at the same time beware of a party spirit that would despise other work and workers or tear them down that we may rise on their ruins. Such zeal is from beneath and not from above. It is contrary to that love which "does not seek its own" (1 Cor. 13:5 NKJV) and looks out not only for one's own interests but "also for the interests of others" (Phil. 2:4 NKJV). Such party zeal will come back like a boomerang upon our own pates and bring ruin upon ourselves.

"For the love of God is broader than the measure of our mind, and the heart of the Eternal is most wonderfully kind."[1] And true zeal makes us like that.

3. The zeal of ignorance. Paul said of his kinsmen, the Jews: "My heart's desire and prayer to God for them is that they may be saved. For I bear them witness that they have a zeal for God, but not according to knowledge. For, being ignorant of the righteousness of God, and seeking to establish their own, they did not submit to God's righteousness" (Rom. 10:1–3 ESV).

True zeal is from above. Its source is in the mountains of the Lord's holiness and its springing fountains in the deep, cool valleys of humility. It is born of the Holy Spirit and flows from a knowledge of "the truth that is in Jesus" (Eph. 4:21 NIV). This knowledge is twofold.

First, it is the knowledge of the dread condition of the soul without Christ—its slavery to Satan, the inherited depravity of its nature, its bondage to sin, its love of it, its enmity toward God (of which the person may be unaware), its guilt, helplessness, ignorance of the way back to the heavenly Father's house and happiness, and its awful danger, if it neglects the offer of salvation and life in Jesus Christ.

Second, it is the knowledge of the unspeakable gift of God, the possibilities of grace for the vilest sinner, the Father's pitying, yearning love. It is the knowledge of sins forgiven, guilt removed, adoption into the Father's family, illumination, consolation, guidance, and safe-keeping. It is the knowledge of depravity destroyed, cleansing through the blood, sanctification by the baptism of the Holy Spirit, salvation from the uttermost to the uttermost, unbroken fellowship with the Father and His Son Jesus Christ through the eternal Spirit, and a life of blessed service and fruit bearing. It is the knowledge of a faith and hope that bear the spirit up over sorrows, trials, losses, pain, and sickness, enabling it at last to cry out in supreme victory and holy triumph, "'O death, where is your victory? O death, where is your sting?' . . . Thanks be to God, who gives us the victory through our Lord Jesus Christ" (1 Cor. 15:55, 57 NASB).

True zeal makes one faithful to Jesus and the souls for whom He died. It led Paul during his three years' appointment at Ephesus "to warn every one night and day with tears" (Acts 20:31 KJV) and to keep back no truth that was profitable for the people, but to show them and teach them "in public and from house to house, testifying both to Jews and to Greeks of repentance toward God and of faith in our Lord Jesus Christ" (Acts 20:20–21 ESV). He was not content simply to get people to accept Jesus as their Savior, but taught them that "this is the secret: Christ lives in you. This gives you assurance of sharing his glory. So we tell others about Christ, warning everyone and teaching everyone with all the wisdom God has given us. We want to present them to God, perfect in their relationship to Christ. That's why I work and struggle so hard, depending on Christ's mighty power that works within me" (Col. 1:27–29 NLT).

Paul was zealous for the perfection in love and loyalty of all his converts, and his zeal led him to seek with all his might to lead them all into this blessed experience. As was Paul, so also was Richard Baxter, who labored indefatigably in spite of lifelong sickness—and at times almost intolerable pain—for the perfection of his people. And so also was John Wesley and George Fox and William and Catherine Booth, and so will be every soul-winner who is full of the zeal of God.

True zeal is sacrificial. Jesus, consumed with zeal for the glory of God in the saving and sanctifying of souls, was led "as a lamb to the slaughter" (Isa. 53:7 KJV). He could say, "I offered my back to those who beat me and my cheeks to those who pulled out my beard" (Isa. 50:6 NLT). He was "despised and rejected of men; a man of sorrows, and acquainted with grief" (Isa. 53:3 KJV). And again, "But he was pierced for our rebellion, crushed for our sins. He was beaten so we could be whole. He was whipped so we could be healed. All of us, like sheep, have strayed away. We have left God's paths to follow our own. Yet the LORD laid on him the sins of us all" (Isa. 53:5–6 NLT).

He poured out His soul unto death for us. He gave His life as a ransom for all. And the gift of His Spirit kindles and sustains this same sacrificial zeal in the hearts of all true soul-winners.

Enlarge, inflame, and fill my heart

With boundless charity divine,

So shall I all strength exert

And love them with a zeal like Thine,

And lead them to Thy open side,

The sheep for whom the Shepherd died.[2]

NOTES

1. Frederick W. Faber, "There's a Wideness in God's Mercy," 1862, public domain.

2. Charles Wesley, "Give Me the Faith Which Can Remove," 1749, public domain.

Spiritual Leadership 5

The soul-winner must have the power of spiritual leadership, and spiritual leadership is a thing of the Holy Spirit, not of birth, rank, title, education, or circumstances.

Joseph was a youthful prisoner in an Egyptian dungeon, but he walked with God and was "a prosperous man" (Gen. 39:2 KJV) because God was with him, and one day he reached his rightful place next to Pharaoh's throne.

Paul was a prisoner under Roman guards on board ship, hastening to Caesar's judgment bar. But one day God's winds made the sea boil, and winds and waves smite the ship, so that the hearts of all the other men on board failed them for fear. Then Paul, by right of spiritual kingship, became the master of all on the ship (see Acts 27).

I knew a Salvation Army lieutenant, a quiet, modest, thoughtful, prayerful, faithful, humble, holy young man of moderate ability. His superiors sat at his feet for spiritual counsel, though the lieutenant knew it not. They hung on his God-wise words, remembered his example, and treasured his spirit. They talked to me about his saintliness and Christlikeness long after he had left them for a flock of his own. They were in charge, but he held spiritual supremacy because he walked with God, and God was with him and in him.

Spiritual leadership is not won by promotion, but by many prayers, tears and confessions of sin, and heart-searchings and humblings before God. It comes by self-surrender; a courageous sacrifice of every idol; a bold, uncompromising, and uncomplaining embrace of the cross; and an eternal, unfaltering looking unto Jesus. It is not gained by seeking great things for ourselves (see Jer. 45:5), but rather by counting those things that once seemed valuable as worthless compared to Christ. Like Paul, I "once thought these things were valuable, but now I consider them worthless because of what Christ has done. Yes, everything else is worthless when compared with the infinite value of knowing Christ Jesus my Lord. For his sake I have discarded everything else, counting it all as garbage, so that I could gain Christ" (Phil. 3:7–8 NLT).

That is a great price, but it must be unflinchingly paid by anyone who would be not merely a nominal but a real spiritual leader, one whose power is recognized and felt in three worlds—heaven, earth, and hell. Moses gained this spiritual leadership among Pharaoh's palace halls and Sinai's solitudes and vastness, when he "refused to be called the son of Pharaoh's daughter; choosing rather to suffer affliction with the people of God, than to enjoy the pleasures of sin for a season; esteeming the reproach of Christ greater riches than the treasures in Egypt" (Heb. 11:24–26 KJV).

Spiritual leaders are not made by human action. Neither conferences, nor synods, nor councils can make them, but only God. Spiritual power is the outcome of spiritual life, and all life—from that of the moss and lichen on the wall to that of the archangel before the throne—is from God. Therefore let those who aspire to this leadership pay the price, and seek the role from God.

Who made Elijah and John the Baptist—hairy, uncouth men of the wilderness and desert—prophets who awed kings and swayed nations? God. Who took Moses from the universities of Egypt and the palaces of Pharaoh and, after drilling him among flocks of sheep in the desert for forty years, made him the meek but unconquerable leader of two million people, and the lawgiver and fountainhead of jurisprudence for all time? God. Who took the baby Samuel and put into his mouth prophetic words to the aged priest, Eli, and made him the spiritual leader of Israel? God. Who took the boy David, trained to feed harmless, patient sheep, put courage into his heart, nerved his arm to fight the lion and the bear and the giant, and gave him skill to lead Israel's armies? And who gave him such skill that the women sang: "Saul has killed his thousands, and David his ten thousands" (1 Sam. 18:7 NLT), while the elders, after Saul's death, came to David, and said, "In the past, when Saul was our king, you were the one who really led the forces of Israel. And the LORD told you, 'You will be the shepherd of my people Israel. You will be Israel's leader'" (2 Sam. 5:2 NLT)? God.

And why did God single out these people and distinguish them, and give them this power above others? Because God was to them the supreme fact. They believed God, sought God, feared and trusted and obeyed God. Read the Psalms and see how God fills the whole heaven of David's thought, desire, and affection, and you will cease to wonder at his leadership. It was based on spiritual life, power, and fellowship with God.

This spiritual leadership, once attained, can be maintained. Witness Moses, Elijah, Paul, Fox, Wesley, Finney, Booth, and ten thousand leaders in humbler spheres who "still bear fruit in old age" and "stay fresh and green" (Ps. 92:14 NIV). They are like a white-haired, old saint of eighty years I once visited who, after I had prayed, burst into prayer also, and said, "O Father, I testify to Thee, and the angels, and these young brothers, that old age is not a time of dotage and second childhood but the springtime of eternal youth."

I hear comparatively young people complaining and expressing fear that when they get old, they will be set aside and superseded by younger people without a tenth of their experience, forgetting that it is not long service and experience that makes spiritual leaders, but vigorous spiritual life, and that if they are set aside, it will be because they have neglected the divine life, the Holy Spirit in them. Nothing can make men and women acceptable leaders, however long their service and varied their experience, if they have lost the spirit of prayer, faith, and fiery-hearted love and the sweet simplicity, trustfulness, and self-sacrifice of their youth, and are now living on past victories, revelations, and blessings. But fresh anointings of the Spirit and present-day experiences will make them acceptable, though their eye be dim, their back bent, and their voice husky with age.

There have been ministers who in their prime fought against the doctrine of holiness and refused the baptism of the Holy Spirit (or who, having received the baptism, neglected and lost it), who filled great pulpits and drew fat salaries but whose influence gradually waned and whose old age was full of complainings and disappointments and bitterness and jealousies, and whose sun went down behind clouds because they neglected God.

But I also know old men and women, full of God, who were persecuted in their prime for Jesus' sake, but who had salt in themselves and kept sweet and delighted themselves in the Lord, whose bow abides in strength (see Gen. 49:24), whose sun shines in fullness of splendor, and who even now fill the world with divine messages that others are eager to hear. Know this, that long service and experience will not save you from becoming obsolete, but God in you will. God is always up to date. And it is God whom people want.

What service had they performed and what experience had Moses, David, Daniel, and Paul when God set them up as leaders? None. But they were in touch with God; they were pliable to His will, teachable, trustful, obedient, courageous, and uncomplaining.

They were full of God. And know this, you who fear the time is coming when your services will no longer be appreciated or wanted and that you will be thrust into a corner, that a man or woman who is full of God cannot be thrust aside. If he is put into a desert place, then all will flock to the desert place, as they did to Jesus and John the Baptist. And if she is thrust into a corner, then the world will stop and bend its ear to her corner to hear the latest message from God. They thrust Paul into prison, but he spoke and wrote words of life and power that burn with the unquenchable fire of the Holy Spirit and are doing more to direct the thought, inspire the faith, and inflame the affections of men and women today than ever before.

The "powers that be" thought they were finished with him when they cut off his head, but after two thousand years his influence goes on increasing.

And so they thought they had silenced Madam Guyon in the Bastille and John Bunyan in Bedford Jail. But who can silence the thunder of God's power or hush His "still, small voice" when He chooses to speak through someone? Their silent prisons become public address systems connected with the skies.

One day, an old man died in one of our large cities. He died long past the age of seventy. He was a minister who, at the age of forty-seven, broke down so utterly in health from overwork that for five years he never read a chapter from a book, not even the Bible. But he held fast his faith in both God and humanity, kept his love all aglow, and at last died full of years and was mourned by hundreds in all parts of the globe who had been saved, sanctified, inspired, and qualified for service by his words and life and the agencies he set in motion for the salvation and sanctification of God's people. And his greatest work was accomplished after he had passed sixty years of age. But while this spiritual power and leadership may be maintained, yet it is a subtle thing that may be lost forever.

When Saul was little in his own sight, he was made king, but when lifted up he became disobedient, and his kingdom was torn from him and given to another. And is it not this we are warned against in the words, "Hold on to what you have, so that no one will take away your crown" (Rev. 3:11 NLT)? The place of Judas among the apostles was given to another (see Acts 1:15–26). The one talent was taken from the "wicked and lazy servant" and given to him who had ten (see Matt. 25:26–28).

I knew a Christian worker who was surrounded by a number of other bright, earnest, teachable, spiritually ambitious young people who looked to him for direction and guidance. He invited them to his home for an evening. While they waited for soul food, coffee and cake were brought out, and when they expected prayer and counsel, the chessboard was produced. The opportunity of the evening slipped away, and the strong bonds that united them in God were relaxed and weakened, if not in one or two cases broken. And, while his official leadership was still recognized, his commanding spiritual leadership was gone, perhaps forever.

"But you, dear friends, must build each other up in your most holy faith, pray in the power of the Holy Spirit, and await the mercy of our Lord Jesus Christ, who will bring you eternal life. In this way, you will keep yourselves safe in God's love" (Jude 20–21 NLT).

Redeeming the Time 6

The soul-winner must value time. Diamonds and gold nuggets are not so precious as minutes. One morning, about five o'clock, John Wesley lost ten minutes through the tardiness of his coachman and mourned for them more than over lost treasure.

Dr. Samuel Johnson tells us, "When [Philipp Melanchthon] made an appointment, he expected not only the hour, but the minute to be fixed, that the day might not run out in the idleness of suspense."[1]

A woman told me that she was sure she got a position as a teacher once by being sharp on time. Another young woman, better fitted for the position, arrived a bit late and remarked, "I thought it wouldn't make any difference if I were a few minutes late." She was politely informed that her services were not wanted, as a teacher had been secured. Eternity is made up of moments, and "lost time is lost eternity."[2]

"Believe me," said William E. Gladstone, "when I tell you that thrift of time will repay you in after life with a usury of profit beyond your most sanguine dreams, and that the waste of it will make you dwindle alike in intellectual and moral stature, beyond your darkest reckonings."[3]

And yet thoughtless idlers try to "kill time," and thus destroy their most valuable possession. What is life but a glad, present consciousness of God and self and duty, and a hearty obedience thereto? But those who kill time seek to forget and would be far better dead.

"The future is nothing but a coming present," wrote Jean Paul Richter, "and the present which thou despisest was once a future which thou desiredst."[4] The philosopher Marcus Aurelius wrote, "Every man lives only this present time, which is an indivisible point, and . . . all the rest of his life is either past or it is uncertain."[5]

If you would redeem the time, begin the moment your eyes open in the morning. Let no idle, foolish, hurtful thoughts be harbored for an instant, but begin at once to pray and praise God and meditate on His glories, His goodness, His faithfulness, and His truth, and your heart will soon burn within you and bubble over with joy. Bounce out of your bed at once and get the start of your work and push it, or else it will get the start and push you. For, "If you in the morning throw minutes away, you can't pick them up in the course of the day."[6]

A fellow Salvation Army officer (minister) said to me one day, "There is much in the habit of work. If a man forms the habit, he naturally turns to it. I find it so with myself. I squander less time now than I once did."

The difference between wise and foolish folks, rich and poor, saints and sinners, redeemed and unredeemed, does not usually result so much from different circumstances and the start they had in life, as it does from the difference in their use of time. One used it purposefully, while the other squandered it. One was a miser of minutes, the other was a spend-thrift of days and months and years. One was always active, packing into every hour some search for truth, prayer to God, communion with Jesus, service to others, counsel to a saint, and warning or entreaty to wandering souls, while the other was neglecting the opportunity of the present but full of vague dreams for an ever receding, elusive future. The one plods patiently and surely to glory, honor, peace, immortality, and eternal life, as the other drifts dreamily, but certainly, into the regions of "indignation and wrath, tribulation and anguish" (Rom. 2:8–9 KJV) and finally lands in hell.

To redeem time one does not mean feverish hurry, but a prompt, steady, quiet use of the minutes. It was said of John Wesley that he was always in haste, but never in a hurry. "Make haste slowly," is a wise old adage.

To save time the soul-winner will find it profitable to go to bed at a reasonable hour and to get up promptly on waking in the morning. Those who have accomplished anything in the world have usually gone to work early in the day. For example, Albert Barnes wrote six-teen volumes in less than an equal number of years, devoting to them only the hours before breakfast.

If you would save time, keep a Bible, notebook, and pencil always at hand. Never go on to the street or take a journey without at least a New Testament with you, and some other useful book if possible. And don't forget to use them. The gospel of Matthew can be read through in approximately two hours. This may not be the most profitable way to read it, and yet it will pay to read it right through at one sitting so as to see the life of Jesus as a whole, as we would the life of anyone. Paul's first letter to Timothy can be read in aboout twenty minutes, while Jude can be easily read in about three minutes.

Catherine Booth had to snatch time from household duties and the care of small children to prepare her marvelous addresses that stirred England and did so much to make and mold The Salvation Army.

The person who sits about smoking and reading novels or whiling away the minutes idly thrumming on a guitar and reading the daily papers will not succeed at soul-saving work. The soul-winner can redeem time by being "instant in season, out of season" (2 Tim. 4:2 KJV) in dealing with others about the things of God.

John Vassar, an eccentric but marvelously successful soul-winner, once saw two women in the parlor of a Boston hotel. He immediately inquired if they were at peace with God, and kindly and earnestly preached Jesus to them, urging them to make ready for death and judgment by accepting Him as Savior and Lord. A few moments later the husband of one of the women came in and found them in tears. He inquired for the reason.

His wife said, "A strange little man has just been talking to us about religion and urging us to get right with God."

"Well," said the man, "if I had been here I should have told him to go about his business."

"My dear," replied the wife, "if you had been here, you would have thought he *was* about his business."

James Brainerd Taylor met a traveler at a watering trough one day, and during the five minutes their horses were drinking he so preached Jesus to the stranger that the man was saved and afterward became a missionary to Africa. They met no more, and the stranger was ever wondering who the angel of mercy was that pointed him to Jesus. One day in Africa he received a box of books. On opening a small volume of memoirs, he saw the picture of the young man who had been about his Father's business and redeemed the time at that watering trough by preaching Jesus and saving a soul, instead of idly chatting about the weather.

It takes no more time to ask people about their souls than about their health, but it will require more love and prayer and holy tact and soul-wakefulness to do it with profit, and these the soul-winner must have.

With many, much time is lost for want of a system. Things are done haphazardly, duties are performed at random, and after one thing is done time is wasted in deciding what to do next. It is well, then, to have a program for every day or, better still, for every hour.

Of course, in this busy world, with its many surprises and unexpected calls, any program must be flexible and not like cast iron, and in times of emergency the soul-winner must be prepared to cast it to the winds and follow where the Spirit leads, singing with the whole heart:

> I would the precious time redeem,
> And longer live for this alone
> To spend and to be spent for them,
> Who have not yet the Savior known,
> And turn them to a pardoning God
> And quench the brands in Jesus' blood.

> My talents, gifts and graces, Lord,
> Into Thy blessed hands receive,
> And let me live to preach Thy Word,

And let me to Thy glory live;

My every sacred moment spend

In publishing the sinner's Friend.[7]

Finally, if you would redeem the time, keep a conscience void of offense and keep your soul red hot with love for Jesus and this dying world. "Have faith in God" (Mark 11:22 KJV). Expect victory. Nothing will sap your energies, dull your faculties, and take from you all incentive to holy and high effort like doubt and discouragement. It is your duty to expect victory.

Joshua, in a fit of discouragement after his army's defeat at Ai, stopped all efforts, fell flat on his face, and stayed there until God came by and said, "Get up! Why do you lie flat on your face like this? Israel has sinned. They have violated my covenant, which I commanded them to keep. They have taken some of the things reserved for me and put them with their own things. They have stolen and kept it a secret. The Israelites can't stand up to their enemies. . . . I will no longer be with you unless you destroy the things reserved for me that are present among you. Go and make the people holy. Say, 'Get ready for tomorrow by making yourselves holy'" (Josh. 7:10–13 CEB).

God wanted Joshua to be up and doing, and if he could not whip the enemy, then he was to clean out his own camp and not be discouraged. Trust God, and trust others. And where others cannot be trusted, love them and pray for them, and you will surely redeem the time and win souls to God.

NOTES

1. Samuel Johnson, "Selections from Dr. Johnson's Rambler," *The Oxford Miscellany* (Oxford: Clarendon Press, 1907), 39.

2. Max Muller, *A Dictionary of Thoughts*, ed. Tryon Edwards (Detroit: F. B. Dickerson Company, 1908), 446.

3. John Morley, *The Life of William Ewart Gladstone*, vol. 1 (London: Macmillan, 2006), 634.

4. Jean Paul Friedrich Richter, *The Campaner Thal and Other Writings* (Boston: Ticknor and Fields, 1864), n. p.

5. Marcus Aurelius, *The Meditations: Book 3*, The Harvard Classics, vol. 2 (New York: P. F. Collier and Son, 1909), 210.

6. Anna Sewell, *Black Beauty* (New York: HarperCollins, 1998), 190.

7. Charles Wesley, "Give Me the Faith Which Can Remove," 1749, public domain.

The Studies of the Soul-Winner **7**

No man or woman need hope to be a permanently successful soul-winner who is not a diligent student of the truth, of the will and ways of God, of souls, and of methods. No one can successfully build a house, write a poem, govern a city, manage a store, or even shoe a horse or make a mousetrap without thoughtful study.

A doctor must think and study—and do so diligently and continuously—in order to understand the delicate human organism, the subtle diseases to which it is subject, and the various remedies by which those diseases are to be cured. A lawyer must be a diligent student if he or she would win cases before judges and juries in the face of self-interest and skillful opponents.

How much more then should the soul-winner study in order to understand the diseases of the soul, the ramifications of evil, the deceitfulness of the human heart, and the application of the great remedy God has provided to meet all the needs of the soul. Or, to change the figure, how must the soul-winner study to win his or her case at the bar of conscience, when the opposing counsel is a deceitful human heart assisted by that old adversary, the Devil, who for six thousand years has been deceiving human souls and leading them down to hell!

Writing to Timothy, Paul said, "Study to shew thyself approved unto God, a workman that needeth not to be ashamed, rightly dividing the word of truth" (2 Tim. 2:15 KJV). He said, "Give attention to reading, to exhortation, to doctrine. Do not neglect the gift that is in you. . . . Meditate on these things; give yourself entirely to them, that your progress may be evident to all" (1 Tim. 4:13–15 NKJV).

Oh, that all who set themselves to be soul-winners might fully recognize the tremendous odds against which they fight and determine by much believing prayer and joyous, diligent study to show themselves to be "approved to God, a workman that need not to be ashamed!" Thank God, none whom God calls need be discouraged or dismayed. Only let them not bury their talents or spend their time in idle dreaming, but let them stir up the gift that is in them and faithfully give a little time each day to those studies that will enlighten the mind and fit them for the work God has called them to, and they shall surely be blessed of God and "thoroughly equipped for every good work" (2 Tim. 3:17 NIV).

The first thing—and the last—to be studied is the Bible. A doctor who knows all about law and art, history and theology, but is unacquainted with medical books, is a failure as a doctor. Likewise, a lawyer who has devoured libraries, traveled the wide world over, and become a walking encyclopedia and dictionary, but is unacquainted with law books, is a failure as a lawyer. So the worker for souls may read ten thousand books, may be able to quote poetry by the mile, may be acquainted with all the facts of science and history, and may even be a profound theologian, but unless that person is a diligent student of the Bible, he or she will not permanently succeed as a soul-winner.

Soul-winners must be full of the thoughts of God. They must eat the Word, digest it, and turn it into spiritual blood, bone, muscle, nerve, and sinew, until they become, as someone has said, "a living Bible, eighteen inches wide by six feet long, bound in human skin."

The evangelist Charles Finney wrote of getting up at four o'clock in the morning and reading his Bible until eight:

I gave myself to a great deal of prayer. After my evening services I would retire as early as I well could; but rose at four o'clock in the morning, because I could sleep no longer, and immediately went to the study and engaged in prayer. And so deeply was my mind exercised, and so absorbed in prayer, that I frequently continued from the time I arose at four o'clock till the gong called to breakfast at eight o'clock. My days were spent, so far as I could get time, in searching the Scriptures. I read nothing else, all that winter, but my Bible; and a great deal of it seemed new to me. Again the Lord took me, as it were, from Genesis to Revelation. He led me to see the connection of things, the promises, the threatenings, the prophecies and their fulfillment; and indeed, the whole Scripture seemed to me all ablaze with light, and not only light, but it seemed as if God's Word was instinct with the very life of God.[1]

This diligent attention to the Word of God is a command. God said to Joshua, "Study this Book of Instruction continually. Meditate on it day and night" (Josh. 1:8 NLT). The object of this earnest study was, "so you will be sure to obey everything written in it." And the result: "Only then will you prosper and succeed in all you do." The blessed life David sang about in Psalm 1 does not come to those who merely refuse to keep company with the ungodly and abstain from their ways, but to those who also "delight in the law of the LORD, meditating on it day and night" (Ps. 1:2 NLT). And the difference between them and the ungodly is the difference between a fruitful tree planted by the river and "worthless chaff, scattered by the wind" (Ps. 1:4 NLT).

Jesus declared the importance of the Word when He told the Devil, "People do not live by bread alone, but by every word that comes from the mouth of God" (Matt. 4:4 NLT).

Catherine Booth read her Bible through a number of times before she was twelve years old. No wonder God made her a "mother of nations." She was full of truth, and she could never open her mouth without saying something that was calculated to expose shams and falsehoods, overthrow the Devil's kingdom of lies, and build up God's kingdom of righteousness and truth in people's hearts.

Whitefield read the Bible through many times on his knees with Matthew Henry's notes. Wesley in his old age called himself "a man of one book."[2] Again and again I have read the Bible through on my knees, and it is ever new and, as David said, "Sweeter also than honey and the honeycomb" (Ps. 19:10 KJV). And like Job I can say, "I have esteemed the words of his mouth more than my necessary food" (Job 23:12 KJV).

It is from this armory that the Christian is to draw weapons with which to fight all hell. It is there that we may study the mind and heart of God, the truth about Jesus Christ, sin and the way of escape from it, and the facts about heaven, hell, a judgment day, and eternity. There we find a law for the lawless, warnings for the careless, promises for the penitent, encouragement for the distressed, balm for the wounded, healing for the sick, and life for the dead. We are to "preach the Word," for it is "useful to teach us what is true and to make us realize what is wrong in our lives. It corrects us when we are wrong and teaches us to do what is right. God uses it to prepare and equip his people to do every good work" (2 Tim. 3:16–17 NLT). And in preaching it, if we preach as they did of old, "in the power of the Holy Spirit sent from heaven" (1 Pet. 1:12 NLT), we will find it "alive and powerful . . . sharper than the sharpest two-edged sword, cutting between soul and spirit, between joint and marrow . . . [exposing] our innermost thoughts and desires" (Heb. 4:12 NLT). I have sometimes read or quoted the Word of God to people, and it fit their case so pat that it smote them like a lightning bolt. "'Does not my word burn like fire?' says the LORD. 'Is it not like a mighty hammer that smashes a rock to pieces?'" (Jer. 23:29 NLT).

But we must not study the Word simply that we may preach it, but that we may live by it, be furnished, strengthened, enlightened, corrected, and made wise by it. It must pass through our own soul and become a part of our own spiritual life before we can preach it with power and apply it effectually to the souls of others. And in order to do this we must be filled with the Holy Spirit. In fact, it is only as we are filled with the Spirit that we will be able to get much benefit from the Word of God or have much love for it.

The Bible is a sealed book to unspiritual people, but when the Comforter comes it is unsealed and its wondrous meaning made clear. I read recently of a lad who could not read receiving the baptism of the Holy Spirit. Then he got his unsaved sister to read the Bible to him and he explained it to her. The Holy Spirit in him enabled him to understand what the Holy Spirit in prophets of old enabled them to write. Only the Holy Spirit can help human hearts and minds to understand His Book.

An old woman loved her Bible very much. A friend who found her reading it frequently gave her a commentary to assist her in getting at its meaning. A few days later, he asked, "How do you like that book I gave you?" She replied, "Oh, that be a very good book, but the Bible do throw a lot of light on that there book."

The Bereans show us the way to read the Bible (see Acts 17:11):

- They received the Word with all readiness.
- They searched the Scriptures. It was not with them just a hasty, careless, thoughtless reading; they searched as prospectors search for gold.
- They did this daily.

Personally, for years I have given the best hour of the day to the Bible, until I want it more than I want my food. It should be read early in the day, before other things crowd in. What is read should be remembered. In eating it is not the amount we eat, but the amount we digest that does us good, and so it is in reading and studying. It is not the amount we read, but what we remember and make our own that does us good.

Besides the Bible, the soul-winner ought to lay out a course of reading, and stick to it, reading a few pages each day. Reading ten pages a day will mean between ten and fifteen books a year, approximately.

Not too much time should be spent reading newspapers. It would probably not be wise to discard them altogether, but better to do that than let them rob you of the time that should be spent in deep study and earnest prayer. I once heard William Booth say, "I have not read a newspaper for ten days."

All useful knowledge may prove valuable to the soul-winner, and we should seek information everywhere. It is well to carry a notebook and constantly make notes.

The soul-winner should study not only books, but also people and methods. John Wesley became a supreme master in practical and experimental theology and a matchless soul-winner largely through his study of people. He examined thousands — men, women, and children — with reference to their religious experience, and especially their experiences of sanctification, until he became acquainted with the human heart and the workings of the Holy Spirit as few have ever done.

I know of no better and surer method of acquainting one's self with the human heart and the way the Holy Spirit works than by this close, personal, private conversation and inquiry about the religious experiences of the Christians around us. This is the scientific method applied to the study of the human heart, the Christian life, and religious experience, and it can be carried on wherever you can find a human being to talk with you. "He who wins souls is wise" (Prov. 11:30 NKJV).

NOTES

1. Charles Finney, *Memoirs of Rev. Charles G. Finney* (New York: A. S. Barnes & Company, 1876), 374.

2. From the preface to Wesley's Standard Sermons, in which he writes, "Let me be *homo unius libri*." *The Works of Wesley*, vol. 1 (Grand Rapids: Francis Asbury Press, 1955), 32.

Physical Health 8

Soul-winners must take the best care they know how of their bodies, without everlastingly coddling, petting, and pitying themselves. This is our sacred duty. The body is the instrument through which the mind and the soul work in this world. A good body is as essential to the Christian as is a good instrument to the musician or a staunch boat to the strong rower, and should be no more despised and neglected than the hunter's gun or the woodsman's axe. "Don't you realize," said Paul, "that your body is the temple of the Holy Spirit?" (1 Cor. 6:19 NLT). He also said, "If anyone destroys God's temple, God will destroy that person" (1 Cor. 3:17 NCV). As the most skillful musician is dependent upon his or her instrument, so we, in every walk of life, are in a large measure limited by and dependent upon the quality of the body through which our mental and spiritual powers must work.

Most people who have made a mark in the world have had a splendid basis of physical force and power (though there are some striking exceptions).

When Moses died on Mount Nebo at 120 years of age, "his eyesight was clear, and he was as strong as ever" (Deut. 34:7 NLT), notwithstanding the fact that for forty years he had the tremendous task of organizing, legislating for, judging, and ruling a great nation of former slaves just delivered from four hundred years of bondage and wandering like sheep in a mountainous wilderness. Paul must have had a robust constitution and fairly good health to have endured the stonings and whippings, imprisonments and shipwrecks, hungerings and thirstings, fights with fierce beasts, and contests with fiercer men, besides the care of all the churches which fell to his lot daily.

John Wesley was a little man, weighing only about 120 pounds, but his health was superb and seems to have been due not so much to natural vigor of constitution—though, doubtless he had that—as to the regular habits and healthful plan of living he adopted. He was one of nineteen children, and his father was a poor clergyman. For several years he had nothing to eat but bread, which may have accounted for his small size, but which he himself said probably laid the foundations of good health he afterward enjoyed. (It must have been whole wheat bread, however, and not the white, starchy stuff of modern bakers.) In after years he always ate sparingly, and only ate a few articles of food at any one meal. He lived much out of doors and preached almost daily (sometimes several times a day) in the open air. At the age of seventy-three he made this remarkable entry in his journal:

I am seventy-three years old, and far abler to preach than I was at three and twenty. What natural means has God used to produce so wonderful an effect?

1) Continual exercise and change of air, by traveling above four thousand miles in a year. [It is well to remember that he did his traveling on horseback and in a buggy through winter's storms and summer's heat.]

2) Constant rising at four.

3) The ability, if ever I want, to sleep immediately.

4) The never losing a night's sleep in my life. [He mentions several all-nights of prayer in his journal, however.]

5) Two violent fevers, and two deep consumptions.

These, it is true, were rough medicines; but they were of admirable service, causing my flesh to come again as the flesh of a little child. May I add lastly, evenness of temper. I feel and grieve; but, by the grace of God, I fret at nothing. But still the help that is done upon earth [God] doeth it Himself; and this He doth in answer to many prayers.[1]

A similar entry was made in his journal in 1782. He said, "I have entered into my eightieth year; but, blessed be God, my time is not 'labor and sorrow.' I find no more pain or bodily infirmity than at five-and-twenty."[2]

And beside the reasons given above he added, "This I still impute, (1) To the power of God, fitting me for what He calls me to do. (2) To my constant preaching, particularly in the morning."[3] The morning sermon was preached at five o'clock in the summer and six o'clock in the winter.

Young people are usually prodigal of their health and strength, and nature will allow them to make large drafts upon these treasures. But nature also keeps strict accounts and will surely require interest and principal in due time. It is a rather remarkable fact that often those who have had poor health in youth so learn to take care of themselves and obey the laws of health and not impose upon their bodies that they outlast and outwork many who started out with a greater physical capital.

Those who desire good health, long life, and a cheerful old age should live simply and regularly. They should seek enough sleep and at the same time be careful not to take too much sleep. Wesley could get along with six hours' sleep at night, though he had the happy faculty of taking naps through the day, even sleeping on horseback. Napoleon frequently got along with three hours' sleep, but General Ulysses S. Grant said that in the midst of his heaviest campaigns he required nine hours. I have heard General William Booth say that he needed eight hours at least. No rule can be laid down to fit every case, however, so that conscientious soul-winners must find out what is best for themselves, make their own rule, and keep it religiously as unto the Lord.

There is a danger of lying in bed too long as well as too short a time. The Duke of Wellington said, "When you find that you want to turn over, you ought to turn out."[4] Lying in bed relaxes the whole system, and if indulged in to excess tends to a general weakening of the system.

Sleep should be taken in a room that is well ventilated in winter as in summer. All good physicians and hygienists insist upon this, and also that one should not sleep in any garment worn during the day.

Benjamin Franklin declared that he had made a great discovery. He discovered that the sun came up in the morning. He thought that it would be a great financial saving to the world if people could only be brought to recognize this fact, and instead of turning night into day by artificial light, should go to bed early and get up with the sun. No doubt there would be many dollars saved and also much nervous energy. We have fallen on evil days, however, and it is not likely we shall ever get back to the habits of our forefathers and go to bed with the birds. Soul-winners, though, ought to conscientiously go to bed as early as possible rather than sitting up and indulging in small talk and late suppers, which if it does not destroy their health will at least greatly injure it and cripple their soul-saving power.

Exercise is also necessary for health. Since the human body, like a chain, is not stronger than its weakest point, a little general systematic exercise is useful to keep every organ of the body in good health and vigor.

On the other hand, those who never relax, however religious they may be, are likely to become morose, irritable, impatient, and a source of anxiety and perplexity to their dearest friends. Or they may become melancholy and full of gloom, and may begin to doubt their call to preach.

There is a legend that when the apostle John was nearly one hundred years of age, he was visited by a man who was anxious to see the "beloved disciple" of the Lord. The man found the old apostle playing with some little children, and he rebuked the aged saint, telling him that it ill-fitted an apostle of the Lord, at his age, to be indulging in childish games. The old man replied, in essence, "A bow that is never unstrung will lose its power; unloose the string and it retains its vigor. So I relieve the tension of my soul by indulging in innocent games with the little ones."

The emotions, sympathies, and every power of mind and soul—along with all the nervous energies of the body—have heavy drafts made upon them in soul-saving work, and the mighty tension of the soul and body at their highest point of efficiency must be entirely relaxed periodically in order to maintain this efficiency. In other words, there must be rest.

I have found that when I get very tired and am least fit to do anything, I then feel an imperative necessity for doing something, and it is then that I must put on the brakes and rest—by sheer force of will, if need be. A friend of mine, who is an unusually successful soul-winner, has a very sensible wife who, when she finds him nervous and worn, insists that he goes to bed for a whole day and vegetates. The next day he finds his nervous force restored and is ready for any amount of hard work.

"Whether you eat or drink," said Paul, "or whatever you do, do it all for the glory of God" (1 Cor. 10:31 NLT). Eating and drinking do not seem to have anything to do with soul-winning, but nevertheless they do. I read recently that three-fourths of the diseases that Americans are afflicted with can be traced to improper eating and drinking. "The fewer the sweetmeats, the sweeter the temper," wrote a wise hygienist. "If you doubt it and have a bad temper, my friend, let me implore you to try it."[5]

Several years ago a friend and I visited Neal Dow, who was sometimes called "the father of prohibition." He was then over ninety years of age and in good health. My friend asked him the secret of his long life and splendid health. The old man replied, "First, I didn't sow any wild oats in my youth; I never used tobacco nor whisky nor stimulants of any kind. Second, I have always gone to bed early, slept well, and gotten up early. Third, I have always taken an active interest in public morals and in the welfare of my fellow men. Fourth, I never eat anything that I have found out by experience hurts me. I am very fond of baked beans, but they do me harm, therefore, I do not eat them." Baked beans may not hurt everybody, but soul-winners who put God's interests and that of other souls before their own pleasure ought to show the good sense of Neal Dow and not eat anything that hurts them, however much they may like it.

I know a minister who was afflicted with gastritis. He wanted some meat for supper; it was on the table in the form of mince pie. He ought to have known, and probably did, that with the kind of stomach he had, mince pie was no diet for him, but he liked it. He ate it, and he nearly died that night. Rich, fatty suppers should not be eaten. Cold bread is preferable to hot bread. It is wise to follow a rule of British prime minister William E. Gladstone: "Give thirty-two bites to every mouthful."[6] That is, give every tooth a taste.

Rev. Daniel Waldo once said, "I am an old man. I have seen nearly a century. Do you want to know how to grow old slowly and happily? Let me tell you. Always eat slowly—masticate well. Go to your food, to your rest, to your occupations smiling. Keep a good nature and a soft temper everywhere."[7]

Dr. J. H. Hanaford, in writing to a public singer who was afflicted with severe congestion and sore throat, said, "I attribute a part of the trouble to using rich pastry, often a prominent cause of catarrh. I suspect in you the too free use of sugar, confectionery, salt, and spices. I am fully convinced that a large percentage of the sore throats, inflamed eyes and nasal passages, and the like, so often attributed to colds, are due to stomach derangement resulting from large quantities of common food, and the too free use of such heating things as sweets, fats and oils, and starches, fine flour being prominent."

Here are some short rules for one who wants good health:

- Don't worry. Paul said, "Don't worry about anything; instead, pray about everything. Tell God what you need, and thank him for all he has done. Then you will experience God's peace, which exceeds anything we can understand" (Phil. 4:6–7 NLT).
- Never despair. Lost hope is a fatal disease. One of the fruit of the Spirit is hope.
- Work heartily, but don't worry yourself to death.
- Court the fresh air day and night.
- Don't overeat. Don't starve. "Let your moderation be known unto all" (Phil. 4:5 KJV).
- Don't forget that "Cleanliness is next to godliness."

Finally, if you have poor health and a broken constitution, don't despair. Richard Baxter, one of the mightiest men of God that ever lived — the Saint Paul and the William Booth of his day — was a lifelong invalid and suffered almost intolerable things. But he praised God for it, for he declared it kept him alive to eternal things, weaned him from the world, and led him constantly to "preach as a dying man to dying men."[8] David Brainerd, the fragrance of whose holy life, apostolic labors, and self-denial have filled and inspired the church for almost two centuries, died of consumption (tuberculosis) before he was thirty years of age. But few men in health and strength have been so used of God as he was in his weakness.

Personally, I have suffered much from broken health, exhausted nerves, and sleepless nights, and at one time feared that my work was done. But by prayer and care I have been so far restored to health and strength that I can work six days in the week with all my might, sleep like a kitten, and digest my food fairly well. I am full of the joy of the Lord, happy as a lark, and am altogether glad I am alive.

> Oh, grant that nothing in my soul
> May dwell, but Thy pure love alone;
> Oh, may Thy love possess me whole,
> My Joy, my Treasure, and my Crown:
> Strange loves far from my heart remove;
> May every act, word, thought, be love.

> Unwearied may I this pursue,
> Dauntlessly to the high prize aspire;
> Hourly within my soul renew
> This holy flame, this heavenly fire;
> And day and night be all my care
> To guard the sacred treasure there.

> In suffering be Thy love my peace,
> In weakness, be Thy love my power;
> And when the storms of life shall cease,
> Jesus, in that important hour,
> In death as life be Thou my guide,
> And save me, who for me hast died.[9]

NOTES

1. John Wesley, *The Works of the Rev. John Wesley in Ten Volumes*, vol. 3 (New York: J. & J. Harper, 1827), 438–439.

2. John Wesley, *The Works of the Reverend John Wesley, A. M.*, vol. 4 (New York: B. Waugh and T. Mason, 1835), 562.

3. Ibid.

4. Source unknown.

5. Rose Seelye Miller, "Some Thoughts on Economy," *The Rushford Spectator* (Rushford, NY), Thursday, October 3, 1889, 3.

6. Source unknown.

7. Daniel Waldo, quoted in "Hear the Old Man," *The R. I. Schoolmaster*, vol. 4 (Providence: William A. Mowry, 1858), 216.

8. Richard Baxter, *Poetical Fragments* (London: J. Dunton, 1689), 30.

9. Paul Gerhardt, "Jesus, Thy Boundless Love to Me," 1653, public domain.

The Renewing of Power 9

To do God's work we must have God's power. Jesus said, "Stay here in the city until the Holy Spirit comes and fills you with power from heaven" (Luke 24:49 NLT). And again He said, "You will receive power when the Holy Spirit comes upon you" (Acts 1:8 NLT).

We receive this power when we are sanctified wholly and filled with the Spirit, and we need never lose it. But while the Holy Spirit abides with the believer, there yet seems to be need for frequent renewals of the power He bestows. And, thank God, He has made ample provision to meet this need. "They that wait upon the LORD shall renew their strength," said Isaiah (Isa. 40:31 KJV). "Wait on the LORD; be of good courage, and He shall strengthen your heart," cried David (Ps. 27:14 NKJV).

Years ago Asa Mahan wrote of his old friend, Charles Finney:

The extraordinary power which attended the preaching of President Finney, during the early years of his ministry, was chiefly owing to a special baptism of the Spirit, which he received not long after his conversion. Hence it was that when, through him, "the violated law spake out its thunders," it did seem as if we had in truth "come unto the mount that might be touched, and that burned with fire, and unto blackness, and darkness, and tempest, and the sound of a trumpet, and the voice of words." But when he spoke of Christ, then indeed did his "doctrine drop as the rain, and his speech distil as the dew, as the small rain upon the tender herb, and as the showers upon the mown grass." The reason, also, why he is bringing forth such wondrous "fruit in his old age," is, that while his whole ministry has been under the power of the Spirit, his former baptisms have been renewed with increasing power and frequency during a few years past.[1]

The need for these frequent renewings and anointings does not necessarily arise from faltering faith. Sometimes the soul feels the need of a renewal of its power when confronted by great opposition, danger, and powerful foes. The apostles were filled with the Holy Spirit, and had not only won their great Pentecostal victory but many others as well when suddenly a stubborn wall of opposition arose before them. They were arrested by the rulers, thrown in prison, brought before the high priest, sharply questioned by what power and name they were working their miracles, and then when no ground for punishment could be found, they were threatened and commanded to preach no more in the name of Jesus.

When they were let go, they went to their own people, told them what had happened, and began a sweet, childlike, heaven-storming prayer meeting. They told the Lord the story too, and cried to Him to show forth His power. Then a wonderful thing happened. Pentecost was repeated: "The meeting place shook, and they were all filled with the Holy Spirit. Then they preached the word of God with boldness. . . . The apostles testified powerfully to the resurrection of the Lord Jesus, and God's great blessing was upon them all" (Acts 4:31, 33 NLT). They waited before the Lord and their strength was renewed, their power reinforced from heaven, their past victories put into the shade, and "a large number of priests became obedient to the faith" (Acts 6:7 NIV).

Sometimes the need for this renewal of strength arises after great victories. Victory is usually secured as the result of great spiritual and mental activity—and often physical activity as well. It is only natural that there should be a reaction. The pendulum, if left alone, swings to the other extreme. Depression may follow, the powers of soul and mind relax, joyful emotions subside, and inexperienced soul-winners may at this point get into great perplexity, suffer from fierce temptation, and strain to keep up their accustomed spiritual activity, crying out with David, "Why am I discouraged? Why is my heart so sad?" (Ps. 42:11 NLT). They may fear that their faith is failing.

But what is needed now is not so much anxious wrestling with God as quiet waiting upon God for a renewal of power, saying to the soul, "I will put my hope in God! I will praise him again—my Savior and my God!" (Ps. 42:11 NLT); "My health may fail, and my spirit may grow weak, but God remains the strength of my heart; he is mine forever" (Ps. 73:26 NLT). At such times the strength of the soul is to

sit still in quietness and confidence (see Isa. 30:15), assured that God
Himself will be its help.

I once heard a wise old evangelist say that while he sat at home
after a season of rest, the Spirit of God would come upon him, leading him to earnest prayer and travail for the salvation of others. This
was God's way of preparing him for a campaign and for victory, and
away he would go for battle and siege, to rescue souls. Never did he
fail to win. But after a while there seemed to be an abatement of
power, when he would return home for another season of rest and
quiet, waiting upon God for the renewal of his strength. And thus he
continued till he was over eighty years old, still bringing forth fruit in
old age (see Ps. 92:14).

There is sometimes need of a renewal of power owing to weakness
and infirmity of the flesh. Paul must have received a great addition of
power when, instead of removing his thorn in the flesh, Jesus said to
him, "My grace is all you need. My power works best in weakness"
(2 Cor. 12:9 NLT). And such was the uplift Paul experienced at that
time that ever afterward he took "pleasure in . . . weaknesses, and in
the insults, hardships, persecutions, and troubles that I suffer for
Christ" (2 Cor. 12:10 NLT), glorying in them, since through them
Christ's power rested upon him, and in weakness he was made strong.

Spiritual power is not necessarily dependent upon physical energy,
and however much soul-winners may be afflicted with infirmities,
there are mighty endowments of power available if they intelligently —
and with quiet and persistent faith — seek them from on high.

There will also be times of loneliness and spiritual agony when
soul-winners will need to have their spiritual strength renewed — such

as Jesus suffered in the garden, or Elijah when he felt that all the prophets were slain and there was none true to God in Israel but himself. When there is widespread barrenness and desolation, when revivals have ceased, when worldliness sweeps in like a flood and there is apparently no vision, when God seems silent, and when the Devil mocks and taunts, a renewal of spiritual strength will be needed—and we may fully expect such a renewal. The angels are all around us, the heavens are bending over us, and Jesus has lost none of His tender interest and sympathy for us in such times. An angel came and strengthened Jesus in His agony, an angel strengthened Elijah for his long and lonely journey, and an angel came to Daniel and said, "O man greatly loved, fear not, peace be with you; be strong and of good courage" (Dan. 10:19 ESV). And not only an angel, but the Lord Himself will surely empower His trusting workers. It was Jesus who cheered Paul in the chief captain's castle (see Acts 23:11) and John on the lonely Isle of Patmos (see Rev. 1:17), and so He still cheers and strengthens His servants and warriors.

These renewals of power are not always necessarily of an extraordinary character. There are sometimes great uplifts of physical strength without any apparent cause, but typically our physical strength will be renewed by rest and the timely eating of proper food. Similarly, there may be times when the Spirit of God falls upon the soul-winner, giving great uplifts and visions and courage. But ordinarily power comes by the use of the simple means of much regular prayer, patient and diligent searching of God's Word, and a daily listening to God's voice. It is renewed like fire, not by the fall of lightning from heaven but by the addition of new fuel, or like physical strength, not by some hypodermic injection of fresh blood but by appropriate food. David called upon his soul to bless God who "satisfies [him] with good things so that [his] youth is renewed like the eagle's" (Ps. 103:5 ESV).

It is by appropriate food, then, that the soul is strengthened. Jesus told us what that food was when He said, "People do not live by bread alone, but by every word that comes from the mouth of God" (Matt. 4:4 NLT). And does not this correspond to Paul's statement that "though our outer self is wasting away, our inner self is being renewed day by day" (2 Cor. 4:16 ESV)? Does it not also align with that passage that says, "The LORD revealed himself unto Samuel in Shiloh by the word of the LORD" (1 Sam. 3:21 KJV)? It is the Lord who renews our strength, but He does it not in some mysterious way but by means of His Word, which we read and meditate upon and appropriate by faith. Through it we see Jesus and come to know our Lord. This will require time and attention on our part, but it will be time well spent.

My own strength is usually renewed by the opening up of some new truth or the powerful application of some promise or portion of the Word of God to my soul, which I am enabled to make my own by a definite and bold act of faith in secret prayer. There is abundant reserve power in God. "The residue of the spirit" (Mal. 2:15 KJV) is with Him. He has not exhausted His resources in the measure of the Spirit of power and holiness which He has given us, and I often comfort and encourage myself with the assurance of James: "He gives us more grace" (James 4:6 NIV). "So let us come boldly to the throne of our gracious God," abide there in communion with God, and "find grace to help us when we need it most" (Heb. 4:16 NLT).

A servant's form He wore,
And in His body bore
Our dreadful curse on Calvary:
He like a victim stood,
And poured His sacred blood,
To set the guilty captive free.

With mercy's mildest grace,
He governs all our race,
In wisdom, righteousness, and love:
Who to Messiah fly
Shall find redemption nigh,
And all His great salvation prove.

Hail, Savior, Prince of Peace!
Thy kingdom shall increase,
Till all the world Thy glory see;
And righteousness abound,
As the great deep profound,
And fill the earth with purity![2]

NOTES

1. Asa Mahan, *The Baptism of the Holy Ghost* (London: Elliot Stock, 1872), 91.

2. Benjamin Rhodes, "My Heart and Voice I Raise," 1787, public domain.

An Undivided Heart 10

The person who hopes to succeed in the infinite business of saving souls with a divided heart as yet knows nothing in comparison to what he or she ought to know concerning the matter.

I admit that someone may by personal magnetism, power or persuasiveness of speech, and a certain skill in playing upon people's emotions create an excitement that fairly simulates a revival, and yet have a divided heart. But that such a person can bring others to a thorough repentance and renunciation of sin, a hearty embrace of the cross, an affectionate surrender to Jesus as a personal Savior and Master who requires deep humility and meekness and tender love as the marks of His disciples is yet to be proven.

As certainly as like begets like, so certainly will the soul-winner put the mark of his or her own spirit and consecration upon the people who are influenced. One who is not more than half won to the cause of our lowly Master will not more than half win others.

Physical scientists manipulate and change dead matter. Journalists seek principally to amuse or interest people for the passing hour. Lawyers and politicians simply seek to change and mold opinions. But soul-winners deal with fundamentals. Their object is not merely to change opinions and conduct, but to change character. Their goal is to work a moral revolution in the affections, dispositions, and wills of men and women—to turn them from temporal things (which they see) to eternal things (which they do not see), from all vices to virtues, and from utter selfishness to utter self-sacrifice, and often in spite of all present self-interest and in the face of the combined opposition of the world, the flesh, and the Devil. Their purpose is not only to save others from the guilt and penalty of sin, but also from the pollution and power and love of sin.

Nor do they aim merely to win souls from sin, which is rather a negative work, but also to usher them into all goodness and love and holiness through a vital and eternal union with Jesus Christ—like that of the branch with the vine—a union that gives perpetual vigor, energy, and fruitfulness in righteousness to all the powers of the soul, filling it with grace and truth.

This is no little work and can never be the work of a divided heart. It is like turning Niagara Falls back upon its source or causing the sun and the moon to stand still on Ajalon. It can be done only by God's power, and that power is only bestowed upon and only works freely in and through those whose hearts are perfect toward Him.

Soul-winners, then, must once and for all abandon themselves to the Lord and to the Lord's work and, having put their hands to the plow, must not look back, if they would succeed in this mighty business. And, if they continue faithful in this way, they shall conquer though they die.

They must love their Lord and love their work, and stick to it through all difficulties, perplexities, and discouragements, and not be given to change, for there is no discharge in this war.

This is where many fail. They do not have a single eye. They make provision for retreat. They are double-minded, like one officer I knew who dabbled in photography till it divided his life and heart and got him out of the ministry, and another minister of whom I heard the other day who reads another man's sermons to his people while he studies law, saying that when he gets a poor appointment he will fall back on the law and leave the ministry. They forget Paul's words to Timothy: "Soldiers don't get tied up in the affairs of civilian life, for then they cannot please the officer who enlisted them" (2 Tim. 2:4 NLT).

Such people eventually leave the work God called them to do, because (as they say) they have not been treated well, when the fact is, their minds being divided, they ceased to work well. They no longer gave themselves wholly to it, and the people feel a lack of interest and power. Hungering souls that looked for bread received a stone. Poor sinners on the road to hell and possibly on the brink of ruin went away from their cold and heartless services unawakened and unchanged. They lost their grip first on God and then on the crowd, and their superiors—perplexed to know what to do with them and where to place them, since the people no longer want them— are blamed. But blame others as they will, the blame still lies with themselves.

No great work has ever been accomplished without abandonment to it. Michelangelo said his work was his wife and the statues he made were his children. Edison was so wedded to his work that all other things were forgotten and set aside in the pursuit of his marvelous inventions.

Demosthenes, the greatest of ancient orators (if not the greatest of all time), was hissed off the platform at his first appearance. His figure was unprepossessing and his voice weak and harsh, but he determined to be heard. He devoted himself to his studies, shaved one side of his head lest he should be led into society, and practiced elocution day and night. To perfect his enunciation, he filled his mouth half-full of pebbles and practiced while climbing a hill, and to successfully contend against the thunders of the Athenian mob, he went to the seashore and strengthened his voice by practicing it against the thunder of the waves.

Lord Beaconsfield stood for parliament five times and at last won his seat. When he first attempted to speak he was laughed from the floor but he sat down, saying, "You will listen to me yet." And they did, when, as prime minister of England, he arbitrated the destinies of Europe.

A great speaker was asked, "How long did it take you to prepare that address?" He replied, "All my lifetime in general, and fifteen minutes in particular."

When Benjamin Franklin, as a poor boy, opened a printing shop, a prosperous competitor said he would drive him out of town. Franklin showed him a piece of black bread from which he dined and a pail of water from which he drank, and asked if he thought a man who could live on fare like that and work sixteen hours a day could be driven out of town. Who knows the name of that competitor, and who has not heard of Franklin?

If those engaged in secular pursuits are given up to their work and consumed with their purpose, how much more should be the soul-winner, who is fighting for righteousness and holiness, for the kingdom of love upon earth, and rescuing souls from the power of sin and the danger of eternal burnings?

If God has set you to win souls, "make no provision for the flesh, to gratify its desires" (Rom. 13:14 ESV). Burn the bridges behind you. Remember Paul's words to Timothy: "Give your complete attention to these matters. Throw yourself into your tasks so that everyone will see your progress" (1 Tim. 4:15 NLT). Let your eye be single. Make no plan for retreat; allow no thought of it. Like Jesus, set your face steadfastly toward your Jerusalem, your cross, your kingdom, your glory, when—having turned many to righteousness—you shall shine as the stars forever and ever (see Dan. 12:3).

You may be ignorant, your abilities may be limited, you may have a stammering tongue, and you may be utterly lacking in culture, but you can have an undivided, perfect heart toward God and the work He has set you to do. And this is more than all culture and education, all gifts and graces of person and brain. If God has bestowed any of these upon you, see to it that they are sanctified and that your trust is not in them. But if He has denied them to you and yet has called you to His service, do not be dismayed; it is not the perfect head but the perfect heart God blesses. For has He not said, "The eyes of the LORD search the whole earth in order to strengthen those whose hearts are fully committed to him" (2 Chron. 16:9 NLT)?

At this point none need fail. And yet, what an awful thing it is that some will fail, and after having prophesied and cast out devils and done many wondrous works in His name, shall hear Him profess, "I never knew you. Get away from me" (Matt. 7:23 NLT).

> Let nothing now my heart divide,
> Since with Thee I am crucified,
> And live to God in Thee.
> Dead to the world and all its toys,
> Its idle pomps and fading joys.
> Jesus, my glory be.[1]

NOTE

1. Charles Wesley, "Come, Jesus, Lord, with Holy Fire," 1880, public domain.

Finance  11

Soul-winners, to be successful, must not be overanxious about finance, but must laugh at the Devil and all his fears, and count God faithful and trust Him to supply all their needs. They should repeatedly read over the last part of the sixth chapter of Matthew, beginning with verse 19. What could be stronger and more positive than the assurance of Jesus that their needs shall be supplied?

When I was a little fellow, I never worried about where my next pair of shoes or my next meal was to come from. My mother did all that worrying, and I trusted her. Jesus says we are not to be anxious about what we shall eat or what we shall wear: "Isn't life more than food, and your body more than clothing?" (Matt. 6:25 NLT). And if God gives you life, will He not give you meat to sustain life? And if He allows you still to live in your body for a season, will He not give you clothing to protect your body? "Look at the birds. They don't plant or harvest or store food in barns, for your heavenly Father feeds them. And aren't you far more valuable to him than they are? . . . So don't worry about these things, saying, 'What will we eat? What will we drink? What will we wear?' These things dominate the thoughts of unbelievers, but your heavenly Father already knows all your needs" (Matt. 6:26, 31–32 NLT).

Jesus would have me trust my heavenly Father as I did my mother. Then I can be a child again, and all I have to do is to pray and obey and trust the Lord, and have a good time before Him, and He will supply my needs and the needs of my little ones whom He has given me. Yes, that is what He means, for He says, "Seek first the kingdom of God and His righteousness, and all these things shall be added to you" (Matt. 6:33 NKJV).

This freedom from anxiety is the privilege and duty of all soul-winners, from carefree workers who have only to get bread for their own mouths to those who have a large family to feed and clothe, and even those with a thousand-fold financial responsibility like Moses or George Mueller or Hudson Taylor or our Salvation Army leaders.

Faith—simple, unmixed faith in God's promise—can no more exist in the same heart with worry than can fire and water or light and darkness consort together; one extinguishes the other. Faith in the plain, unmistakable promise of God, begotten by the Holy Spirit, so links the soul-winner to Jesus, so yokes and unites him or her in partnership together, that the burden and care is the Lord's, since the cattle on a thousand hills and the silver and the gold are His (see Ps. 50:10; Hag. 2:8). And He would have His children trust Him, walk the waves with Him, never doubt Him, shout the victory through Him, and triumph over all fear and all the power of the Enemy in Him. According to the Word of God this is His will for the soul-winner, and a secret every true soul-winner must and does know.

God does not send soul-winners to a warfare at their own charges, but according to Paul, "shall supply all [their] need according to his riches in glory by Christ Jesus" (Phil. 4:19 KJV).

God's supply depot is abundantly full and runs on time, but the worried and anxious unbeliever wants Him to run ahead of schedule. No, no! He may, in order to test and strengthen faith, not provide the second suit until the first one is ready to be laid aside, and sometimes after supper He may allow you to go to bed not knowing where the breakfast is to come from, but it will come at breakfast time. "Your heavenly Father already knows all your needs" (Matt. 6:32 NLT), so trust Him, as does the sparrow. The wee thing tucks its tiny head under its little wing and sleeps, not knowing where it will find its breakfast, and when the day dawns it chirps its merry note of praise, and God opens His great hand and feeds it. And "you are of more value than many sparrows," said Jesus (Matt. 10:31 ESV). The psalmist said, "The eyes of all look to you in hope; you give them their food as they need it. When you open your hand, you satisfy the hunger and thirst of every living thing" (Ps. 145:15–16 NLT).

Trust Him! He will not fail you. In this, as in all other things, the assurance holds well that "the temptations in your life are no different from what others experience. And God is faithful. He will not allow the temptation to be more than you can stand. When you are tempted, he will show you a way out so that you can endure" (1 Cor. 10:13 NLT). I have proved this in times past, and I may have to prove it again, but "God is faithful" (and the Devil is a liar and always will be).

Finney's clothes got threadbare, but he was so intent on getting souls saved that he didn't notice it until someone came along and measured him for a new suit. I had a similar experience once. God knew when the old suit needed replacing by a new one, and He sent it along on time.

Many people lose their love for souls and their power to win them by allowing covetousness or financial anxiety to crowd childlike trust out of their hearts. The Lord cried to the backslidden, covetous prophets of old, "Who is there even among you that would shut the doors for nought? Neither do ye kindle the fire on mine altar for nought" (Mal. 1:10 KJV). They would do nothing until they knew they would be well paid for it. It was not souls but money they worked for.

Contrast that with Paul's unselfish, disinterested devotion. He said, "I have never coveted anyone's silver or gold or fine clothes. You know that these hands of mine have worked to supply my own needs and even the needs of those who were with me. And I have been a constant example of how you can help those in need by working hard. You should remember the words of the Lord Jesus: 'It is more blessed to give than to receive'" (Acts 20:33–35 NLT).

He also said, "I seek not yours but you" (2 Cor. 12:14 KJV). He even went so far as to say, when they gave him anything, "Not [that] I desire a gift: but I desire fruit that may abound to your account" (Phil. 4:17 KJV). It was not the benefit he derived from receiving so much as the benefit they would derive from giving that rejoiced his heart.

In writing to the Philippians, who had sent him a donation, he revealed a bit of his inner experience. He said, "How I praise the Lord that you are concerned about me again. I know you have always been concerned for me, but you didn't have the chance to help me. Not that I was ever in need, for I have learned how to be content with whatever I have. I know how to live on almost nothing or with everything. I have learned the secret of living in every situation, whether it is with a full stomach or empty, with plenty or little. For I can do everything through Christ, who gives me strength" (Phil. 4:10–13 NLT).

And writing to Timothy, Paul said that a leader in the church must "not love money" (1 Tim. 3:3 NLT), while Peter said we are to "shepherd God's flock . . . because you are happy to serve, not because you want money" (1 Pet. 5:2 NCV).

In all this I do not contend that God would not have soul-winners amply supported and relieved of financial burden and care by the people for whom they give their lives. God says, "Those who work deserve their pay" (Luke 10:7 NLT) and He forbade the muzzling of the ox that trod out the corn (see Deut. 25:4). And by the tithing system, which all Christians ought to adopt, everyone was to assist in the support of the ministry.

But what I do contend is that soul-winners must not be anxious about their bread. They must beware of covetousness. They must seek to save souls, and if those souls do not support the soul-winner as one might wish, must still love them unto death, seek their salvation, and cheerfully and triumphantly trust the God who fed Elijah and rained manna from heaven for forty years to feed a million Israelites to find a way to provide. I maintain against all devils and all unbelief that God will not disappoint, but will satisfy you with the finest of wheat, "more than the richest feast" (Ps. 147:14; 63:5 NLT).

Kings shall fall down before Him,

And gold and incense bring;

All nations shall adore Him,

His praise all people sing;

For Him shall prayer unceasing

And daily vows ascend;

His kingdom still increasing,

A kingdom without end:

O'er every foe victorious,

He on His throne shall rest;

From age to age more glorious,

All blessing and all blessed.

The tide of time shall never

His covenant remove;

His name shall stand forever,

His changeless name of Love.[1]

NOTE

1. James Montgomery, "Hail to the Lord's Anointed," 1821, public domain.

Saving Truth 12

All truth is precious, but not all truth is adapted to secure the immediate salvation and sanctification of souls, any more than all medicine is adapted to cure heart disease or rheumatism. There are certain truths which, preached in the power of the Holy Spirit, are as much adapted to save and sanctify souls as food to satisfy hunger or fire to melt ice. There are other truths, equally biblical, that will no more secure such results than the truths of the multiplication table will comfort a brokenhearted mother while mourning her lost children or the facts of astronomy will quiet a guilty conscience roused from the slumber of sin.

Some time ago I read the amazing and humbling statement that "there were over three thousand churches in two of the leading denominations of this country that did not report a single member added by profession of faith last year." Well may the writer add,

"Think of more than three thousand ministers in two denominations world-renowned for their schools and culture, preaching a whole year, and aided by deacons and Sunday school teachers and Christian parents and church members and prayer meetings and helps and helpers innumerable, and all without one soul added to God's kingdom!"

Why this stupendous failure? It cannot be that truth was not preached and taught in the Sunday schools and prayer meetings. These preachers and teachers and parents were orthodox, cultured, and skilled in biblical lore. No doubt they preached and taught truth from one end of the year to the other, but it was not *the truth*—the truth that saves, the truth that first smites the conscience, lays bare the secrets of the heart, and arouses the slumbering soul until, self-convicted, it feels that everyone it meets is acquainted with its guilt, every wind and every footfall is an accusing voice, and no cover can hide it from God's searching eye. And when conviction has wrought its purpose and penitence is complete, saving truth whispers of forgiveness and peace, and offers mercy and salvation full and free through the bleeding Lamb of God, "before the world's foundation slain."[1] Such truth preached faithfully and constantly in these pulpits and churches— with power and authority, like thunderbolts from the cannon's mouth—might have set the nation ablaze with revival fire.

The fact is, there are different kinds or grades of truth for different classes of people, just as there are different medicines for various diseases and food for different ages and constitutions. Jesus declared this when He said, "There is so much more I want to tell you, but you can't bear it now" (John 16:12 NLT). The soul-winner must recognize this fact, and seek rightly to divide the word of truth (see 2 Tim. 2:15).

The follower of Jesus needs a different kind and application of truth from that needed by those who are far from God, and the sanctified man or woman can receive the strong meat of God's Word, while babes in Christ must be fed on milk (see 1 Cor. 3:1–2; Heb. 5:12, 14).

With skeptics or seekers, the principal appeal should be made to the conscience and the will. They may be moral, and more or less amiable in their family and social relations, and honorable among their business associates. But be sure that under this is secret selfishness and heart sin—seeking their own way, disobedient to the light, careless to the dying love of Jesus, and in reality if not in profession, enemies of God (see Rom. 8:7). They must be acquainted with these facts, and faithfully and lovingly and firmly warned of their utter ruin if they do not repent. Repentance—deep, thorough, and heartfelt—leading to a confession and an utter, eternal renunciation of all sin and a complete amendment of life and a making right (as far as possible) of all past wrong must be presented as the "strait gate" through which they can enter the highway to heaven. We must insist on an immediate and unconditional surrender to all the light God gives, and offer them mercy and tender love through Jesus Christ when they yield.

The motives that lead to repentance are drawn from eternity, and there is a whole armory of truth with which wandering souls can and must be bombarded to bring them to terms. Truth such as the certainty that what they sow they shall reap, that their sins will surely find them out, that death will speedily overtake them, and that if, refusing mercy, they presume on the goodness of God and continue in selfishness and sin, hell shall be their portion forever. Truth that a life of peace and joy here, a happy deathbed, and eternal glory can be offered as the alternative, on condition of obedient faith.

Very much the same kind of truth is necessary for souls that have strayed or turned from the faith, except that the proportions may have to be varied. If they are stubborn, thunder the law at them until they hoist the white flag and sue for mercy. If they are sorrowful but fear it is vain to try again, then they should be encouraged in every possible way to look up and trust; the infinite love and pity of God revealed in Jesus should be pressed upon their attention, and they should be urged to cast themselves upon God's mercy.

If these foundational truths of repentance toward God and faith in our Lord Jesus Christ are faithfully, affectionately, and prayerfully presented, and the wandering or wayward soul grasps and trusts them, that soul will be accepted by the Lord and adopted into His family. They must then be fed upon truths different from those they were fed on before. They will have tender hearts, and so it will be most unwise to thunder the law at them, though they should be fully instructed as to the spirituality of the law, and that it is the law by which God wishes us to order our conduct and for which abundant grace will be given. Nor should they now be asked to surrender—since they did so when they gave their lives to Christ—but should be intelligently instructed as to the nature and extent of the consecration that is expected of them, and should be urged, and wisely and tenderly encouraged, to make this consecration, presenting their bodies as living sacrifices and yielding themselves to God, "as those that are alive from the dead" (Rom. 6:13 KJV).

They should then be instructed as to the fact of inbred sin, which they will soon find stirring within themselves, and the importance and possibility of having this enemy cast out. Holiness should be presented not so much as a stern demand of a holy God but rather as the glorious privilege of the beloved child of God. They should be taught that it is an experience in which "perfect love expels all fear" (1 John 4:18 NLT), a rest of soul in which—as our bones and sinews are covered with skin and thus unseen—the fact of duty, while still remaining in force, is clothed and hidden by love.

Therefore, while the necessity of holiness should be presented, and a gentle and constant pressure brought to bear upon the will, yet the principal effort should be made to remove slavish fear by opening up the understanding, and so drawing out the confidence and affections that the soul—which in conversion bowed at the feet of Jesus as its conqueror—shall now intelligently and rapturously yield to Him as its heavenly Bridegroom. The heart should be moved to fall so desperately in love with Him by the incoming of the Holy Spirit that it shall cry out with David, "I delight to do your will, O my God" (Ps. 40:8 ESV) and with Jesus, "My food is to do the will of him who sent me" (John 4:34 ESV).

If we as soul-winners do not keep a clear, warm, tender experience of full salvation ourselves, there is a danger of driving the people to a legal experience instead of leading them into the experience of "perfect love." A legal experience is one in which we brace up to our duty because the law demands it, in which we are prodded and pushed up to it by the terrors of the law rather than led up to it by the sweet wooings and gentle drawings of love.

When skeptical, seeking, and straying souls are present in a holiness meeting (church service), there will be a strong temptation to address them. But, as the kind of truth they need differs from that needed by Christians, confusion is likely to result if this is done, and an uncertain experience may be engendered in the hearts of those who love God. In such meetings, it will usually be found wisest to go straight for the Christians, to get them sanctified. The Lord has been pleased to give me victory along this line, and I usually find that some souls nonetheless seek salvation in my holiness meetings (church services).

Jesus likens a Christian to a sheep. Our duty, then, in the holiness meeting is not to club them with the law but rather to feed them with the promises and assurances of the gospel, teach them to discern the voice of the Good Shepherd, and remove all fear so that they may gladly follow Him. The staple diet of all saints should be the promises, seasoned with the commandments to give them a healthy relish.

The promises draw us on in the narrow way, and the commandments hedge us in so that we do not lose the way. The promises should be so presented, and the fullness there is in the gospel and in Jesus so brought to view, that the souls of the people will run hard after Him and not need continual beatings to keep them from breaking through the hedge onto the Devil's territory.

To clearly discern and skillfully apply the truth needed by the souls that surround us requires heavenly wisdom, and well did Paul exhort Timothy, "Be a good worker, one who does not need to be ashamed and who correctly explains the word of truth" (2 Tim. 2:15 NLT). But our work will be in vain unless we, in lowliness of mind, sit at the feet of Jesus, seek wisdom from God, and submit ourselves in glad, prayerful faith to the Spirit of truth who can and will guide "into all truth" (John 16:13 KJV).

The Bible, which contains the revealed truth necessary to salvation, will surely puzzle and mystify all who come to it in the big and swelling conceit of worldly wisdom, but it will open its treasure to the plain and humble heart who comes to it full of the Spirit that moved holy men of old to write it.

O Lord, evermore give to Your people leaders and teachers filled with the Spirit and clothed with His wisdom!

> Happy the men to whom 'tis given,
> To dwell within that gate of heaven,
> And in Thy house record Thy praise;
> Whose strength and confidence Thou art,
> Who feel Thee, Savior, in their heart,
> The Way, the Truth, the Life of grace.
>
> Better a day Thy courts within
> Than thousands in the tents of sin;
> How base the noblest pleasure there!
> How great the weakest child of thine!
> His meanest task is all divine,
> And kings and priests Thy servants are.[2]

NOTES

1. Johann Andreas Rothe, trans. John Wesley, "Now I Have Found the Ground Wherein," 1727, public domain.

2. Charles Wesley, "How Lovely Are Thy Tents, O Lord," 1798, public domain.

Keeping the Flock 13

Soul-winners must give much time, thought, prayer, and effort to the keeping and strengthening of those who come to faith through their efforts. They ought to say with Paul, "It gives us new life to know that you are standing firm in the Lord" (1 Thess. 3:8 NLT). Also like Paul, they should pray earnestly night and day, asking God to supply whatever is lacking in the faith of new Christ-followers (see 1 Thess. 3:10). Paul's ambition was not simply to get people into God's kingdom and united with some local church, but to "present them to God, perfect in their relationship to Christ" (Col. 1:28 NLT).

There is a danger of spending far more effort and care in getting people to the point of commitment than in keeping them after they are there. After a baby is born, it must be intelligently and constantly cared for, or it will very likely die. Soul-winners are not spiritual incubators, but fathers and mothers in the faith, with all the measureless responsibility not

only of leading souls to faith in Christ, but also of keeping them after
they come to faith.

William Booth once said to a few of us who were traveling with
him, "Look well to the fire in your own souls, for the tendency of fire
is to go out." And yet a fire will never go out if it is frequently well
shaken down and fresh fuel is added. We must look well to the spark
of fire kindled in the hearts of new Christians and fan it gently but
surely to a flame and help them to care for it, that it may never go out.
The saddest thing in all this mighty work of soul-winning is the fact
that in so many instances the fire does go out, the light ceases to shine,
the salt loses its savor, and souls that were redeemed and washed with
the precious blood of Jesus—that have been made "partakers of the
Holy Spirit, and have tasted the good word of God and the powers of
the age to come" (Heb. 6:4–5 NKJV)—fall away and return to their old
sins, like "the dog . . . to his own vomit" and the "sow that was washed
to her wallowing in the mire" (2 Pet. 2:22 KJV).

Judas fell from the very face and ministry of Jesus Himself. On
another occasion, after one of Christ's searching sermons, we read that
"many of his disciples turned away and deserted him" (John 6:66 NLT).

Paul mourned the loss of Demas, who "loved this present world"
(2 Tim. 4:10 KJV). He foresaw and foretold the backsliding of some of
the Ephesian church leaders (see Acts 20:29–30), and after his mighty
victories there, which radiated to all the surrounding nations, he had
to write sorrowfully to Timothy, "As you know, everyone from the
province of Asia has deserted me—even Phygelus and Hermogenes"
(2 Tim. 1:15 NLT). "Things that cause people to trip and fall into
sin must happen," Jesus said (Luke 17:1 CEB), and backslidings will

follow. But soul-winners must strive mightily against this, until, like Paul, they can appeal to their people and say, "I declare today that I have been faithful. If anyone suffers eternal death, it's not my fault, for I didn't shrink from declaring all that God wants you to know" (Acts 20:26–27 NLT). They must not only win souls, but must also keep them.

They must be visited. Some time ago I visited a Salvation Army corps (church) in California. The officer (pastor) met me at the train, and on the way to my lodgings remarked, "We got one of the worst drunkards in town saved last night, and I have seen him twice this morning and he is doing well." Of course he would do well with such love and care as that! If they cannot be visited at once, drop them a note and enclose a suitable tract.

A businessman of about fifty years of age, together with his wife, came to faith in Christ in one of my meetings. In a subsequent meeting, I missed him, so I wrote him a note telling him I was praying for him. The next night he was present and told how he had been sorely tempted, but that note blessed him and helped him to get the victory. He became a good Salvation Army soldier (member). In all probability, it was that timely little note, written in five minutes and costing only the price of a postage stamp, that kept him from falling.

They should be encouraged to read their Bible daily, together with other good books. When I was in Boston, I went to the Bible Society and got them to donate forty little New Testaments, one of which I would give to each new Christian, after having marked a number of helpful texts and written his or her name on the flyleaf. Years afterward I was visiting a corps when a young man asked me if I remembered him. I did not. He pulled out a little, well-worn Testament, pointed to his name, and asked if I knew that writing. I did.

"You gave me this Testament years ago," he said, "when you were captain in Boston. I have kept it and read it ever since, and am to be enrolled as a soldier tonight."

They must be taught to pray and urged to practice regular and frequent secret prayer, until they know its sweetness and inexpressible necessity and profit. They must be instructed to keep believing, and also made to see the difference between sin and temptation.

They should be patiently encouraged to work for others, especially for their own people. The Bible says, "Andrew went to find his brother, Simon, and . . . brought Simon to meet Jesus" (John 1:41–42 NLT), and new followers of Jesus must do likewise.

They should be patiently, tenderly, firmly led into the experience of sanctification or (as it is otherwise known) perfect love. They must not be allowed to stop at consecration, but must be pressed on into a definite experience of full salvation. It was at this point that Asa Mahan said his friend Charles Finney failed during his early ministry. He was unexcelled in getting people to a complete renunciation of all sin, to making right all past disobedience, and finally to a complete consecration of all to Jesus. He would start them off for the future with vows to obey God at all points, while nothing was said to them about trusting Jesus to cleanse their hearts at once and fill them with the Holy Spirit. Our vows are only ropes of sand until the Holy Spirit has come with consuming fire into our hearts, filling them with perfect love. Mahan wrote:

No individual, I believe, ever disciplined believers so severely, and with such intense and tireless perseverance, on that principle, as my brother Finney, before he learned the way of the Lord more perfectly.

Appalled at the backslidings which followed [his] revivals, his most earnest efforts were put forth to induce among believers permanence in the divine life. In accomplishing this, he knew of but one method—absolute and fixed renunciation of sin, consecration to God, and purpose of obedience. (Not a word about the faith that receives.) During his pastorate in [New York], for example, he held for weeks in succession special meetings of his church for perfecting this work, and never were a class of poor creatures carried through a severer process of discipline than were these. Years after, as their pastor informed me, those believers said they had never recovered from the internal weakness and exhaustion which had resulted from the terrible discipline through which Mr. Finney had carried them.

When he came to Oberlin and entered upon the duties of his professorship, he felt that God had given him a blessed opportunity to realize in perfection his ideal of a ministry for the churches. He had before him a mass of talented and promising theological students, who had implicit confidence in the wisdom of their teacher and with equal sincerity would follow his instructions and admonitions. He accordingly, for months in succession, gathered together those students at stated seasons, instructed them most carefully in regard to the nature of the renunciation of sin, consecration to Christ, and purpose of obedience required of them.

Then, under his teachings and exhortations, they would renew their renunciations, consecrations, and purposes of obedience, with all the intensity and fixedness of resolve of which their natures were capable. The result, in every case, was one and the same—not the new life of joy, and peace, and power that were anticipated, but groaning bondage under the law of sin and death. At the commencement, and during the progress of each meeting, their confessions and renunciations, their solemn consecrations and vows of obedience, were renewed, if possible, with fuller determination than ever before. Each meeting, however, was closed with the same dirge songs: "Look how we grovel here below"; "Where is the blessedness I knew, when first I saw the Lord?"; or "Return, O Holy Dove, Return."

And as they went out, not their songs of joy and gladness were heard, but their groans became more and more terribly audible. "They followed," and followed hard, "after the law of righteousness, but did not attain to the law of righteousness. Wherefore? Because they sought it not by faith, but as it were by the works of the law"; that is, by self-originated efforts and determinations.[1]

Thank God, Finney learned better, and soul-winners should profit by his example. New followers of Jesus Christ must utterly renounce sin, make wrong things right, and consecrate themselves fully to the Lord to obey Him in all things great and small. But they must understand fully that that is only *our* part, and that they must now wait on their heavenly Father and believe for Him to do *His* part, which is to cleanse their hearts and fill them with the Holy Spirit. They must continue in glad, believing, wrestling, never-give-in prayer, till the Comforter comes into their hearts in all His cleansing, sanctifying, and comforting power. They must tarry in Jerusalem till they are endued with power from on high (see Luke 24:49). They must believe God and receive the Holy Spirit, remembering that God is more willing to give the Holy Spirit to them that ask Him than parents are to give good gifts to their children (see Luke 11:13). That is so. I have proved it.

Soul-winners should so organize their work and train their people that they shall have wide-awake, willing workers to assist them in looking after the new believers. It will take patience and tact and prayer to train these workers, but it will abundantly repay all effort. "To every man his work" is the inspired plan (Mark 13:34 KJV).

Moses had such helpers (see Ex. 18:21–26) and Paul depended much on such help (see 2 Tim. 2:2; Titus 1:5). But there must not be too many irons in the fire. Everything must be subordinated to this one end of saving souls and making them into valiant soldiers of Jesus Christ. Paul said, "This one thing I do" (Phil. 3:13 KJV).

Organization must not be overdone, lest the workers become like David in Saul's armor, lest their power be exhausted in routine and they become like a mighty engine that has not sufficient power to run itself. Let the machinery be simple, and the divine, Holy Spirit power be abundant. For this there must be much prayer and patient waiting upon God. The power is His and can be had when persistently, believingly, humbly, and boldly applied for.

To succeed in getting people to work harmoniously together we must be melted or heated by a great common passion, and welded together like two pieces of iron, until there is no longer Greek or Jew, Englishman or Irishman, French or German, American or European, "but Christ is all, and in all" (Col. 3:11 KJV). Love is the only thing that will do this, and love will do it. I heard one of our officers say, "I got saved in a Salvation Army meeting where I could not understand a word spoken. But the love of Jesus was there, and I understood that."

In cold weather, people of all nations will gather around a stove in which there is a fire, and so they will gather around men and women who are full of love. Love "binds us all together in perfect harmony" (Col. 3:14 NLT), according to Paul. It quenches jealousies, destroys envyings, burns up suspicions, begets confidence, and holds people together with bonds stronger than death. Let us have it and have it more abundantly. More love, more love, more love! Without it we are nothing.

We may be gifted in speech and song as are the angels. We may be shrewd and far-seeing and able to accurately forecast the future. We may be encyclopedic in our knowledge. We may have mountain-moving faith. We may be charitably inclined and feed and shelter many poor to the extent of using up all our resources and wearing out our bodies, but if we have not the gentle, holy, humble, longsuffering, self-forgetful, unfailing, unsuspicious, self-sacrificing, generous, lowly love of Jesus, we are nothing. We are as sounding brass and tinkling cymbal (see 1 Cor. 13:1–8).

It was this love that enabled Paul to write, "I will not be burdensome to you: for I seek not yours but you. . . . And I will very gladly spend and be spent for you; though the more abundantly I love you, the less I be loved" (2 Cor. 12:14–15 KJV). And here is another bit of Paul's autobiography that ought to be put on every soul-winner's wall throughout the land, every word of which is freighted with the love that filled his great heart:

You yourselves know, dear brothers and sisters, that our visit to you was not a failure. You know how badly we had been treated at Philippi just before we came to you and how much we suffered there. Yet our God gave us the courage to declare his Good News to you boldly, in spite of great opposition. So you can see we were not preaching with any deceit or impure motives or trickery.

For we speak as messengers approved by God to be entrusted with the Good News. Our purpose is to please God, not people. He alone examines the motives of our hearts. Never once did we try to win you with flattery, as you well know. And God is our witness that we were not pretending to be your friends just to get your money! As for human praise, we have never sought it from you or anyone else.

As apostles of Christ we certainly had a right to make some demands of you, but instead we were like children among you. Or we were like a mother feeding and caring for her own children. We loved you so much that we shared with you not only God's Good News but our own lives, too.

Don't you remember, dear brothers and sisters, how hard we worked among you? Night and day we toiled to earn a living so that we would not be a burden to any of you as we preached God's Good News to you. You yourselves are our witnesses—

and so is God—that we were devout and honest and faultless toward all of you believers. And you know that we treated each of you as a father treats his own children. We pleaded with you, encouraged you, and urged you to live your lives in a way that God would consider worthy. For he called you to share in his Kingdom and glory. (1 Thess. 2:1–12 NLT)

And again he said, "I kept back nothing that was profitable unto you, but have shewed you and have taught you publicly, and from house to house. . . . I am pure from the blood of all men. For I have not [neglected] to declare unto you all the counsel of God. . . . Therefore watch, and remember, that by the space of three years I ceased not to warn every one night and day with tears" (Acts 20:20, 26–27, 31 KJV).

This is the love that will build up new believers, and nothing else will. We must have love, love, love! We must look for love, pray for love, believe for love. We must exercise love ourselves and inspire all our people to love, and then they will watch over one another, and pray and weep for each other, and bless one another, and be united as one, and the gates of hell cannot prevail against us.

Oh, that we all, as soul-winners, may have melting baptisms of holy love that shall make us like Jesus—patient, gentle, faithful, courageous, tireless, undismayed, and utterly unselfish. Then shall our spiritual children abound and be strong. If we do not have this love, God will give it to us in answer to persistent, believing prayer. He surely will. I do believe.

NOTE

1. Asa Mahan, *Autobiography: Intellectual, Moral, and Spiritual* (London: T. Woolmer, 1882), 246–247.

Saving the Children 14

Not only did Jesus say, "Let the little children come to me, and do not hinder them" (Mark 10:14 NIV), but He also gave to Peter the positive command, "Feed my lambs" (John 21:15 NLT). In that command, He laid a responsibility upon soul-winners for the children, "for the kingdom of God belongs to such as these" (Mark 10:14 NIV). In no other field and among no other class can soul-winners work with such immediate success and such far-reaching results.

Children are not hard to reach with the gospel, if the soul-winner will merely be simple and use common sense in dealing with them. They are not hardened in sin; their consciences are tender, their hearts open, their minds receptive, their wills pliable, and their faith simple. They are keenly alive to the love of Jesus, the glories of heaven, the terrors of hell, and the omnipresence of God. They learn readily to pray in faith about everything and to cast all their care upon God. No eyes are so keen as theirs to see the Light that enlightens everyone, no hands are so ready to do His bidding, and no feet so ready to run in His ways.

And yet effort must be put forth ceaselessly to win them and keep them after they are won, for the corruption of their own natures, the evil example and teaching of a hostile world, and the wiles of the vigilant and tireless Enemy of all souls will soon blind their eyes and harden their hearts and utterly ruin them, if they are not soon won to Jesus and filled with His love. You may feel yourself unfitted for this task, but if God has called you to be a worker for souls it is your business to fit yourself for it.

The first thing necessary is to believe in the possibility of the conversion of the children. Certainly the plain teachings of Jesus, the examples found in the Bible, and the multitude of examples that anyone with open eyes can see ought to convince the most skeptical person of this possibility.

Almost from Samuel's babyhood the Lord spoke to him and filled his heart and mind with wisdom, so that none of His words fell to the ground (see 1 Sam. 2:26; 3:1–21). God ordained Jeremiah from childhood to be a prophet to the nations, and filled him with His Spirit (see Jer. 1:5–10). If this was possible under the law, how much more gloriously is it possible under the gospel? Catherine Booth experienced salvation when she was a child and William Booth as a mere lad, and all their sons and daughters were but children when they were brought to the Savior.

Jonathan Edwards, in one of his works, tells of a wee girl, not even five years of age, going to and from her bedroom looking most sad and disconsolate. Her mother asked her what was the matter, and the little thing replied, "Mama, when I pray God doesn't come." The mother tried to comfort her, but her little heart was filled with hunger that only the Comforter Himself could satisfy, and she still continued to go disconsolately to her bedroom. But one glad day she ran from her room, leaped into her mother's bosom, threw her arms around her neck, and cried, "O Mama, Mama, when I pray now, God comes!" And up through the years of her childhood and youth and womanhood she lived such a life of Christian humility and grace and truth as was the wonder of all who knew her.[1]

Secondly, since they can be won, you must make up your mind that you will win them. You must put from your mind forever the thought that "anything will do for the children." It will require much prayer, patience, love, tact, and divine wisdom to win them to the Savior and to keep them after they are won. They must have "line upon line . . . precept upon precept" (Isa. 28:13 NKJV). If one teaching of the lesson is not sufficient, then they must be taught it again and again.

"Why do you tell Charles the same thing twenty times over?" asked the father of John and Charles Wesley of their mother. "Because nineteen times won't do," replied the wise and particular mother.

Moses said:

Listen, O Israel! The LORD is our God, the LORD alone. And you must love the LORD your God with all your heart, all your soul, and all your strength. And you must commit yourselves wholeheartedly to these commands that I am giving you today. Repeat them again and again to your children. Talk about them when you are at home and when you are on the road, when you are going to bed and when you are getting up. Tie them to your hands and wear them on your forehead as reminders. Write them on the doorposts of your house and on your gates. (Deut. 6:4–9 NLT)

This was the way the children of the ancient Israelites were to be taught, and this must be the standard soul-winners set for themselves and their people today.

The children should be noticed, and I am increasingly convinced that in every meeting where children are present something should be said that is suitable to them, and the invitation to come to Jesus should include them.

When they do come, they should be dealt with most thoroughly. Their little hearts should be probed, their sins searched out, and thorough repentance required. Their fears must be tenderly removed by showing them the fullness of God's love and the certainty of salvation when they give up sin. Their thoughts should be turned to Jesus and their faith fixed on Him and grounded in His Word. Give them His sure promises, such as, "If we confess our sins to him, he is faithful and just to forgive us our sins and to cleanse us from all wickedness" (1 John 1:9 NLT). Above all, you must be simple and make things very plain for the children. They don't know the meaning of many big words that you understand quite well, so you must take pains to make yourself understood.

The other day I was talking to some children, and I gave them this text: "Remember now your Creator in the days of your youth" (Eccl. 12:1 NKJV). I asked them if they knew what the word *Creator* meant, and none of them knew. Neither did they know what the word *youth* meant. So I had to explain that the text meant that they were to remember and think about God and love Him while they were little boys and girls.

I also gave them the text, "Behold, how good and pleasant it is when brothers dwell in unity!" (Ps. 133:1 ESV). But none of them knew the meaning of the word *unity*. One said that it meant "home," and that was a pretty good guess. But I had to explain that the text meant that it was good and pleasant for little brothers and sisters—and big ones, too—to live together in peace, without quarreling and fighting. They all understood that.

You will have to put on your thinking caps and set your brains to work to make your teaching simple for the children. But love will help you.

Some time ago I heard a youth worker singing lustily to a lot of children: "Get your baggage on the deck and don't forget to get your check . . ."[2]

But he didn't explain that it simply meant that they were to give themselves to Jesus, throw away their sins, and be sure to get His love in their hearts. So when he got through I felt sure that there was nothing but a confused rattle of "baggage, deck, check, quick," in the ears of the children, with no useful or saving idea in their little heads and hearts.

If you pray to God for wisdom and love, He will help you to make the deepest spiritual truths plain to the children. As I simplify my talks God gives me the joy of seeing many young people seeking Him for salvation, and I have occasionally seen some gloriously sanctified.

Some time ago, in one of my meetings, I had a penitent form (the kneeler in front of the church) full of children, with each of whom I dealt personally. I asked one little fellow, "What are you here for, darling?"

"To get saved," said he.

"Get saved from what?" I inquired.

"From my sins."

"And what are your sins?"

"I fight," and then he broke down and cried.

"And what are you here for?" I asked a little girl.

She, too, said she was there to "get saved," and I asked what her sins were. She hesitated a little and then said, "I'm cruel to my sister and brother." And then she broke down and cried.

Another little girl said that she swore, and another said she disobeyed her mother. One little boy confessed that he told lies. Another said he smoked cigarettes, and yet another said he was disobedient to his teacher. And so they told of their sins, broke down and wept, and prayed and asked God to forgive them and make them good. And I believe that most of them entered God's kingdom.

In another meeting a little fellow of ten got sanctified and filled with the Spirit, and had all fear taken out of his heart—where before he had been very timid—because, said he, "Jesus is with me now." In another meeting a little girl, about ten years of age, got sanctified. She lived a holy life for about three years and then died happy, sending me word beforehand that the Lord still sanctified her and was keeping her to the end.

But after we have done all, we must remember that they are only lambs, not sheep. We must not forget that they are growing children, not grown men and women. They are in the formative state, tender and inexperienced, and life and the world are full of interest to them. They have a personality and individuality of their own, and are not always willing to take the simple word of their elders, nor to yield to admonition and instruction, but desire to prove their own powers and to taste and see all things for themselves. Therefore it will be necessary not only to talk much to them about God—and even more so—but also to depend upon the mighty, constant cooperation of the Holy Spirit in securing their salvation and keeping them in the grace of our Lord Jesus Christ.

We must show all diligence in our efforts until, if possible, we can at least say to them as Paul said to Timothy: "You have been taught the holy Scriptures from childhood, and they have given you the wisdom to receive the salvation that comes by trusting in Christ Jesus" (2 Tim. 3:15 NLT).

Blessed Jesus, *save* our children!
Be their Guardian through life's way;
From all evil e'er protect them,
Walk Thou with them, come what may.
In white raiment let us meet them
When earth's shadows flee away.

Blessed Jesus, *lead* our children
Into paths of service sweet;
Up the hill of Calvary climbing,
May they and the sinner meet!
More than conquerors, let us see them
Bring their jewels to Thy feet!

Blessed Jesus, *make* our children
Thine for life and thine for aye!
When death's waters overtake them,
Be their Rock, their Light, their Stay!
Tender Shepherd, let us find them
On Thy breast in realms of day![3]

NOTES

1. Summarized and paraphrased from *The Works of Jonathan Edwards, A.M.* (London: William Ball, 1834), 361–362.

2. Based on the song, "De Gospel Raft," *Minstrel Songs, Old and New* (Boston: Oliver Ditson & Co., 1883). This wording was used in the song "Hideaway" in a 1921 recording by Oscar Ford.

3. Emma Booth-Tucker, "Blessed Jesus, Save Our Children," formerly in *The Salvation Army Songbook*; quoted in Frederick St. George de Lautour Booth-Tucker, *The Consul: A Sketch of Emma Booth Tucker* (London: The Salvation Army Publishing Department, 1904), 99. Emphasis added.

Saving the Children 15
(Continued)

Rough-and-ready Peter, that old fisherman, thought he was cut out for and best fitted to be a prime minister, secretary of state, or bishop, and it seems had several disputes with the other disciples in which he suggested that perhaps he should be considered the greatest among them (see Mark 9:34, Luke 9:46). How surprised he must have been, then, when he got his commission from Jesus to be a youth worker and received orders to feed the lambs! What a mighty argument he could have made to prove that he was not fitted for work with children! To be sure, he had at least one boy of his own (see 1 Pet. 5:13), and maybe several others, but he was a fisherman, and the care of the children was largely left to his wife. In fact, he had no fitness either by nature or training for that kind of work. All his associations had been with the big, burly men of the sea, and what did he know about talking to children? All his thoughts and desires and ambitions ran in another direction, and was he not too old and set in his ways to change now?

But Jesus, with infinite knowledge, wisdom, and tenderness, looked straight into Peter's eyes and asked him that searching question, "Do you love me more than these?" (John 21:15 NLT). And when in reply to his answer, "Yes, Lord . . . you know I love you," Jesus said, "Feed my lambs," what could Peter say? So Peter was first commissioned to be a worker among the little ones.

"But," you say, "didn't Jesus mean new Christians, when He said, 'My lambs'? And might they not be men and women who had only recently experienced new life in Christ?" True, it is probable that Jesus meant new Christians, but that company includes children. And didn't Jesus say, "for the kingdom of God belongs to such as these" (Mark 10:14 NIV)? So, however we may explain the text, we cannot escape the fact that Peter was commanded to work with and for the children. And if Peter, why not you and I? Are we not commanded to look well to the flock over which the Holy Spirit has made us shepherds (see Acts 20:28)? And was there ever a flock in which there were no lambs? If so, it was a flock doomed to speedy extinction.

Are we not commanded to do with our might what our hands find to do (see Eccl. 9:10)? And do we not find multitudes of little ones un-shepherded, unloved, untaught, and for whose tender little souls no one cares, prays, or weeps before the Lord, and whose little hands are stretched out toward us, saying, "Come, and help us"? Shall we wait until they are old in sin, hardened in wickedness, fixed in unholy habits, and bond slaves of the Devil before we work and plan and pray for them and seek their salvation?

Is it possible that we have a call to the work of saving souls and yet have no commission for the children? No, no, no! To every worker who says to Jesus, "Lord, You know I love You," Jesus says, "Feed my lambs." We may feel that we have no fitness, no tact, no skill, and no gifts for that kind of work, but the commission lays upon us the responsibility to study and think and watch and pray and love and believe and work ourselves into fitness. And by beginning with just such poor, feeble, untrained gifts as we have; by making the most of every opportunity; by being diligent and faithful; by having courage and pluck and good cheer and faith; and by seeking God's blessing day by day, this fitness can surely be attained.

The poor, struggling soul who never dreamed he had any music in his soul or in his fingers until he encountered Jesus at a Salvation Army penitent form, but who sets himself to it and patiently thrums away at a guitar or blows at a cornet for six months or a year until he can play fairly well, can with equal diligence, patience, determination, and attention learn to interest and bless and help the children. But he must put his heart and soul into it.

I read some time ago of a minister who was sure he was called and fitted only to preach big sermons to big folks. But one day he heard a fellow minister talk so instructively and entertainingly to the children that he determined to acquire that gift, and by thought and prayer and practice he, too, became a powerful children's worker.

Go and do likewise.

Do you ask, "How can I become such a worker?"

1. Make up your mind that you ought to do so and that by God's grace you will. Then make it a matter of daily prayer and thought and meditation. Above all, seek help from God.

2. Get all the help you can from others. Study their methods, but don't become a vain imitator of anyone. Be yourself.

3. Study the best books you can find on the subject. There are many bright books that will greatly help you.

4. Try to put yourself in the place of the child, and ask what would interest you. Make things plain and simple. Watch for illustrations and anecdotes that interest children, and which they can understand.

5. Above all, have a heart full of tender love and sympathy for the little ones, and you will be interesting and helpful to them whether you can talk much or not. They will feel your love and respond to it, and so you can point them to Jesus and help them in their first timid steps toward heaven.

When in the slippery paths of youth
With heedless steps I ran,
Thine arm unseen conveyed me safe,
And led me up to man.

Through hidden dangers, toils, and deaths,
It gently cleared my way;
And through the pleasing snares of vice,
More to be feared than they.

When worn with sickness, oft hast Thou
With health renewed my face;
And when in sins and sorrows sunk,
Revived my soul with grace.

Ten thousand thousand precious gifts
My daily thanks employ;
Nor is the last a cheerful heart
That takes those gifts with joy.

Through every period of my life
Thy goodness I'll pursue:
And after death, in distant worlds,
The glorious theme renew.[1]

NOTE

1. Joseph Addison, "When All Thy Mercies, O My God," 1712, public domain.

Tact 16

Recently in my regular Bible reading I came to that tender appeal of King David to his generals as they were going forth to fight with Absalom: "Deal gently for my sake with the young man, even with Absalom" (2 Sam. 18:5 KJV), and my heart was touched with its likeness to Jesus.

Absalom was in rebellion against his father, David the king, had driven his father from his throne, had outraged his father's marital ties, had sacrificed filial affection and trampled upon duty, and was now seeking his father's life. But David knew Absalom only as his wayward boy, loved him still, and commanded his warriors to deal gently with him in the coming battle. He would have the rebellion crushed, but the rebel saved; the sin destroyed, but the sinner rescued.

How like Jesus that is! Is not that the way Jesus feels toward the most desperate, careless sinner? Does not His heart yearn over them with unutterable tenderness? And is not this written for our admonition? Does He not say to us, "Deal gently for My sake"?

The battle went against Absalom that day, and hardhearted, willful, stubborn old Joab slew him deliberately in spite of the king's wish. And so it often is today. Joab's tribe has increased, and while Jesus would have wayward souls dealt with gently, Joab rises up and thrusts them through with reproaches and bitter words and sharp looks, slays them utterly, and Jesus' heart is broken afresh, as David's heart was.

The elder brother in the story of the prodigal son (see Luke 15:11–32), with his ungenerous jealousy and cruel words and hardness of heart, grieved the loving old father as surely as did the prodigal with his riotous living.

There are many reasons we should deal gently.

We should deal gently with people that we may be like Jesus. When Peter denied Jesus and cursed and swore, Jesus loved him still—and turned and gave him a tender look that broke his heart—and Peter went out and wept bitterly. And after the resurrection Jesus did not rebuke and reproach Peter, but tenderly asked him, "Do you love me?" (John 21:15 NLT) and then commissioned him to feed His lambs and sheep.

Should we, then, who at our best are only sinners saved by grace, despise our Lord's example and deal roughly with His sheep that have gone astray? Since He has freely forgiven us our tremendous debt, shall we not forgive our brothers and sisters (see Matt. 18:23–35)?

We should deal gently with them lest we ourselves grieve the Spirit and falter in faith. Paul wrote to the church in Galatia, saying, "Dear brothers and sisters, if another believer is overcome by some sin, you who are godly should gently and humbly help that person back onto the right path. And be careful not to fall into the same temptation yourself" (Gal. 6:1 NLT). I have noticed that when professing Christians act harshly toward those who falter it is usually only a question of time when they themselves fail—in fact, it is pretty certain that they are already losing faith in their hearts. In the very act of killing the rebellious Absalom, Joab himself rebelled against the expressed wish and command of his king, though he did it under the cloak of loyalty.

And so those today who are severe in their dealings with others under the cloak of zeal for righteousness and loyalty to truth are themselves rebelling against the example and spirit of Jesus, and unless they repent, the world shall surely soon witness their fall.

We should deal gently that we might win back wayward souls. Jesus loves them still, seeks them continually, and waits to forgive, cleanse, and restore to them the joy of salvation the moment they return, and we must not hinder, but help. But we shall not do so unless we deal gently. Harsh dealing would not win us, nor will it win them.

Paul wrote to Timothy, "A servant of the Lord must not quarrel but must be kind to everyone, be able to teach, and be patient with difficult people. Gently instruct those who oppose the truth. Perhaps God will change those people's hearts, and they will learn the truth. Then they will come to their senses and escape from the devil's trap. For they have been held captive by him to do whatever he wants" (2 Tim. 2:24–26 NLT).

This gentleness is not inconsistent with great firmness and unswerving loyalty to the truth. In fact, it is only when it is combined with these sturdy virtues that it commends itself to the judgment and conscience of wrongdoers, and is likely to really win them from the error of their ways.

Firmness of manner may unite with great gentleness of spirit. I may be as tender in spirit in warning and commanding my child to beware of the fire as I am in soothing him after he is burned.

While harshness and severity will only harden the wanderer from God on the one hand, a gospel of gush will fill Him with indifference or contempt on the other. The soul-winner, then, must not have the hardness and brittleness of glass or cast iron, nor the malleability of wrought iron or putty, but rather the strength and flexibility of finest steel that will bend but never break, that will yield and yet retain its own form.

It is generally true that holy mothers have more influence with and win more willful boys and girls than do the fathers—not because the mothers are more ready to compromise principle and sacrifice truth, but rather because while unwavering in their fidelity to righteousness, they mingle mercy with judgment and a passion of gentle, unfailing love and most tender solicitude with firmness and loyalty to the claims of God's perfect and holy law.

But how shall one who has not this spirit of perfect gentleness secure it? There is but one way. It is a fruit of the Spirit, and is to be had only at Jesus' feet.

Jesus is like a "Lamb slain" (Rev. 13:8 KJV)—mutely gentle—and yet again He is "the Lion of the tribe of Judah" (Rev. 5:5 KJV)—firm and strong. He combines the strength of the lion with the gentleness of the lamb.

You, then, who would have His Spirit, confess your need. Are you hard, harsh, critical, severe, and unrelenting? Tell Him and ask Him to destroy this carnal mind and give you His mind. And as you ask, believe, for "anything is possible if a person believes" (Mark 9:23 NLT).

To maintain this spirit you must walk in the footsteps of Jesus and feed on His words. Only to those who seek Him day by day with the whole heart, and with joy, is it given to be like Him in these heavenly tempers and dispositions. "Let this mind be in you, which was also in Christ Jesus" (Phil. 2:5 KJV).

What though a thousand hosts engage,
A thousand worlds, my soul to shake?
I have a shield to quell their rage,
And drive the alien armies back;
Portrayed it bears a bleeding Lamb;
I dare believe in Jesus' name.

Me to retrieve from Satan's hands,
Me from this evil world to free,
To purge my sins and loose my bands,
And save from all iniquity,
My Lord and God from heaven came;
I dare believe in Jesus' name.[1]

NOTE

1. Charles Wesley, "Surrounded by a Host of Foes," 1749, public domain.

How to Speak 17

Thank God for such preachers and such preaching as are spoken of in the Bible, where we read, "At Iconium Paul and Barnabas went as usual into the Jewish synagogue. There they spoke so effectively that a great number of Jews and Greeks believed" (Acts 14:1 NIV)! How did they do it? What was their secret? I think it was threefold.

1. Their manner. They must have won the multitude by the sweetness, grace, persuasiveness, and earnestness of their manner. They certainly did not offend and shock them by coarse, vulgar, uncouth speech, or by a weak and vacillating, light and foolish, or boisterous and domineering manner. They wanted to win souls, and they suited their manner to their purpose.

Solomon said, "Whoever loves a pure heart and gracious speech will have the king as a friend" (Prov. 22:11 NLT). This "gracious speech" is not a thing to be despised. It is rather something to be thought about, prayed over, and cultivated. It was said of Jesus, "Everyone . . . was amazed by the gracious words that came from his lips" (Luke 4:22 NLT). Soldiers said of Him, "We have never heard anyone speak like this" (John 7:46 NLT). Undoubtedly this graciousness was not only in what He said, but also in the way He said it. His manner was authoritative yet gentle, strong yet tender, and dignified yet popular and familiar. You can say to a little child, "Come here, you little rascal," in such a sweet manner as to win his or her confidence and draw him or her to you. You can also say, "Come here, you darling child," in such a rough, coarse way as to fill him or her with fear and drive him or her from you. It is largely a question of manner.

David Garrick, the great actor, was asked why he could move people so mightily by fiction, while preachers, speaking such awful and momentous truths, left them unmoved. He replied, "[They] speak truth as though it were fiction, while I speak fiction as though it were truth."[1] It was a question of manner.

A woman who was so far away from the evangelist George Whitefield that she could not hear what he said was weeping. A bystander asked her why she wept, since she knew not what he said. "Oh," said she, "can't you see the holy wag of his head?" His manner was matchless. Lawyers pleading before judges and juries, and political speakers seeking to win votes cultivate an ingratiating manner. Why, then, should not we who are seeking to win souls to Jesus Christ seek from God the best manner in which to do this?

2. Their matter. I judge that not only was the manner of Paul and Barnabas agreeable and attractive, but their subject matter was interesting and inexpressibly important. They preached the Word. They

reasoned out of the Scriptures. They declared that the prophecies were fulfilled; that Jesus Christ, the Son of God, of whom Moses and the prophets wrote and spoke, had come, was crucified, was buried, but was risen again; and that through obedient faith in Him, men and women might have their sins forgiven, their hearts purified, and their whole being sanctified and filled with God. It was not stale platitudes they preached, or vain babblings about this or that ritual or tradition, or harsh criticisms of authorities and "powers that be," or divers and strange doctrines, but it was "repentance toward God, and faith toward our Lord Jesus Christ" (Acts 20:21 KJV). This was the substance of their message.

It was a joyful message. It was good news. It was a declaration that God was so interested in humanity and "so loved the world that He gave His only begotten Son, that whoever believes in Him should not perish but have everlasting life. For God did not send His Son into the world to condemn the world, but that the world through Him might be saved" (John 3:16–17 NKJV). This war-worn, sorrowful old world needs such a joyful message.

It was an illuminating message. It showed them how to be delivered from sin and made acceptable to God. It also threw a flood of light into the grave and beyond, and "brought life and immortality to light" (2 Tim. 1:10 KJV), proclaiming Jesus as the "first of a great harvest of all who have died" (1 Cor. 15:20 NLT). Their message robbed earth of its loneliness and the tomb of its terrors. It turned the world into a schoolroom and preparation place for the Father's house of many mansions, and made heaven real.

It was a solemn and searching message. It called men and women to remember their sins and repent of them, forsake them, and surrender themselves no longer to the pleasures of ease, but to the service of God. They must take sides. If they would experience salvation, they must follow Christ crucified. Every road leads two ways: If they would put away sin and follow Jesus, He would lead them to heaven, but if they rejected Him they would surely go their own way to damnation, to hell.

3. Their spirit. A speaker's manner may be acceptable and the message true but if his or her spirit is not right, there will not be a "great number" who believe. The cannon may be a masterpiece and the powder and shot perfect, but if there is no fire, the enemy need not fear. The manner may be uncouth and the message fragmentary and faulty, but if the spirit is right—if it is humble and on fire with love—believers will be won.

When Cataline, a Roman citizen, conspired against the state, the matchless Roman orator Cicero delivered a series of orations against him. The people were captivated by the eloquence of Cicero. They went from the Forum praising his oratory, lauding his rhetoric, extolling his gestures, and exalting his graceful management of the folds of his toga.

However, when Philip of Macedon was planning to invade the states of Greece, the Athenian orator Demosthenes delivered a series of orations against him, and the Greeks went from his presence saying, "Let us go and fight Philip!"

Undoubtedly the manner and matter of the two orators were equally above criticism, but they were as far apart as the north and south poles in spirit. One sent the people away talking glibly and prettily about himself, while the other sent them away filled with his spirit and fired with a great impulse to die, if necessary, fighting the invader.

I imagine it was this right spirit, this white heat of soul, this full-orbed heart-purpose that was the principal factor in winning that multitude of believers in Iconium that day. Paul and Barnabas were great believers themselves. They were full of glad, triumphant, hell-defying and hell-defeating faith. They were not harassed by doubt and uncertainty. They did not preach guesses. They knew whom they believed (see 2 Tim. 1:12), because they believed they spoke (see 2 Cor. 4:13), and they so spoke that the faith of a multitude of others was kindled from the fire of theirs.

This faith had also kindled in their hearts a great love. They believed the love of God in giving His Son for them, and their hearts were in turn filled with love for Him. They believed the dying love of the Savior, and their hearts were so constrained with love for Him that they were prepared to die for Him. They believed the love of God for all, until they loved like Him, felt themselves debtors to all, and were ready to be offered as a sacrifice for the salvation of others.

Oh, it was a bright faith and a burning love that set the spirits of those two men on fire! And I think this Christlike spirit molded their manner and made them natural and gentle and strong and true and intense with earnestness, with no simper or whine or affectation of false pathos, no clang of hardness, no sting of bitterness, and no chill of heartless indifference. What school of oratory can touch and train the manner of an actor so that he or she shall for an instant compare with the untrained, shrinking parent who is suddenly fired with a quenchless impulse to plead for the life of his or her child? The best teacher of style in public speech is a heart filled to bursting with love for Jesus, and love, hope, fear, and faith for others. A love that makes a speaker feel that souls must and shall be won from hell and turned to righteousness and heaven and God will surely, in due time, make the manner effective.

And it will also shape and control, if it does not make, the message. It is pitiable to see what flat, insipid, powerless, soulless messages people can manufacture when their faith is feeble and their hearts are cold. But it is marvelous what messages people get whose hearts are afire. Someone asked why the evangelist William Bramwell could say such wonderful things. The reply was, "He lives so near the heart of God and the throne that he gets secret messages and brings them down to us."

Can we not, then, sum up for ourselves the secret of Paul and Barnabas in the words of Solomon: "Guard your heart above all else, for it determines the course of your life" (Prov. 4:23 NLT)?

NOTE

1. Charles Henry Mackintosh, *The All-Sufficiency of Christ*, Miscellaneous Writings of C. H. Mackintosh, vol. 1 (New York: Loizeaux Brothers, 1898), n. p.

After the Meeting 18

A Salvation Army soldier (church member) said to a friend of mine recently, "Our captain [pastor] is good in a meeting; he is a fine talker. He does lay it down to the sinners and the people—sinners and all—like him." But then, after some time, she came back to the subject and said, "Our captain is so light and trifling after the meetings that many are the blessings I get in the meetings and lose afterward through his light talk and jokes and carrying on."

Did the captain wear a mask during the meeting while warning, entreating, and pleading with souls, and take it off after the meeting? Is it possible for someone to be in earnest for the salvation of souls while the meeting is going on and yet become thoughtless and careless as soon as the people are dismissed? Is a soul-winner a mere weather vane blown about with the wind? Or is he or she a person of principle who feels as jealous for the glory of God and as burdened for the salvation of others off the platform as on it? What do you think?

Successful soul-winners used to leave the meetings with serious faces and anxious hearts, and go home to pray and often weep before the Lord if souls were not saved. And I know some like that today. O Lord, revive us again and still pour out on us that Spirit!

It depends on us, each of us for him- or herself, whether or not we will have that Spirit. Others know whether we have it or not. And we are judged, measured, and rewarded, not by what we say on the platform only, but also by what we say and do, and by the spirit we manifest off the platform.

"Be an example to the believers," said the apostle (1 Tim. 4:12 NCV). "Be sober" (1 Pet. 5:8 KJV).

Do not despair if you are given to foolish talking and joking, but seriously set yourself to get the victory over it. The next time you come off the platform in a jesting mood, thank God for showing it to you, then stop and pray for deliverance at once, and He will give it to you. I know a woman who got a lasting victory in that way, one that has been abiding for nearly a score of years.

Do not understand, however, that there should never be any pleasantry in your words or acts. But such should be controlled by the Holy Spirit, that those who got a blessing in the meeting shall not lose it, but rather have it increased after the meeting.

'Tis not the time to rest at ease
When men are dying fast,
And hastening onward to their doom
That's evermore to last.

Then let us work while yet 'tis day,
For night will quickly come,
And then we'll hear the Master say—
"Ye faithful ones, well done!"[1]

NOTE

1. Author unknown, "Upon the River's Brink They Stand," *Salvation Army Songs* (London: The Salvation Army Book Department, 1911), 464.

Dangers the Soul-Winner Must Avoid 19

Sanctification floods the soul with great light and love, and thus subjects the possessor to two great and opposite temptations and dangers.

If we lean to the side of light, we are likely to become critical and faultfinding, impatient with others, too severe in our judgments and requirements of those who may yet be in comparative darkness. And thus, unlike our Lord, we may break the bruised reed that Jesus would not break and quench the smoking wick which Jesus would fan into a flame, and so fail to "faithfully bring forth justice" (Isa. 42:3 ESV). Sanctified people see the way so clearly that they are tempted to think that everyone else should so see it, and that it is only because they *will not* that they *do not*. It will be helpful for us to remember "the quarry from which [we] were dug" (Isa. 51:1 ESV), our own darkness and weakness and slowness (if not obstinacy and waywardness), and to be as merciful and patient in our judgments and criticisms of others as our Lord has been with us. If we do not seek earnestly to do this, we are in awful danger.

On the other hand, if we lean to the side of love, we are likely to be too lenient, too easy (as was Eli with his sons), using soothing ointments when we should wield a sword. Many a work of God has come to naught that might have been saved by a timely, courageous rebuke and faithful dealing.

To keep in the middle of the way—to walk in a blaze of light without becoming critical and harsh and spiritually proud and overbearing, and in fullness of love without being soft and weak and fearful of offending—is the problem every sanctified soul must solve in order to keep the blessing and be increasingly useful.

Not to err on either side will require great humility of mind, courage, firmness, faith, watchfulness, prayer, constant meditation on the work and ways of God, and a patient, trustful waiting on the Lord for the wisdom and leading of the Holy Spirit. Blessed is the one who walks with God in the middle of the way, without falling into the ditch on either side.

On Thee, O God of purity,
I wait for hallowing grace;
None without holiness shall see
The glories of Thy face.

Lead me in all Thy righteous ways,
Nor suffer me to slide,
Point out the path before my face;
My God, be Thou my guide!

All those that put their trust in Thee,

Thy mercy shall proclaim,

And sing with cheerful melody

Their great Redeemer's name.

Protected by Thy guardian grace,

They shall extol Thy power,

Rejoice, give thanks, and shout Thy praise,

And triumph evermore.[1]

NOTE

1. Charles Wesley, "On Thee, O God of Purity," 1743, public domain.

PART TWO

Love Slaves

Love Slaves 1

James, Jude, Peter, and Paul—in an age when labor and service were a badge of inferiority and shame—wrote boldly and proudly as follows: "James, a servant of God and of the Lord Jesus Christ" (James 1:1 NIV); "Jude, a servant of Jesus Christ" (Jude 1 NIV); "Simon Peter, a servant and apostle of Jesus Christ" (2 Pet. 1:1 NIV); "Paul and Timothy, servants of Christ Jesus" (Phil. 1:1 NIV); "Paul, a servant of God" (Titus 1:1 NIV).

That age with its false standards and corrupt glories was doomed and dying, and those early followers of Christ stood on the threshold, ushering in a new era in which service was to become a badge of loyalty and a distinguishing mark of the children of God and the citizens of heaven upon earth. The word *servant* as used by them meant a slave. They counted themselves slaves of God and of Christ.

The word and the relationship seems harsh and forbidding, but not so when we realize its meaning to these apostles. They were love slaves. The bondage that enthralled them was the unbreakable bondage of love.

There was a law among the Hebrews that for sore poverty, debt, or crime, one man might become the servant of another, but he could not be held in servitude beyond a certain period; at the end of six years he must be allowed to go free (see Ex. 21:1–6; Deut. 15:12–17). But if he loved his master and preferred to remain with him as his slave, then the master was to place the man against a door or doorpost and bore a hole through his ear. This was to be the mark that he was his master's servant forever.

It was not the slavery of compulsion and law, but the willing and glad slavery of love. And this was the voluntary attitude of Paul, Jude, Peter, and James. Jesus had won them by love. They had sat at the feet of the great Servant of love, who came not to be served but to serve, to minister to others, and to give His life as a ransom for all (see Matt. 20:28). They had seen Him giving Himself to the poor, the weary, the heavy laden, the vile, the sinful, and the unthankful. They had seen His blessed life outpoured:

> Like the rush of a river,
> Wasting its waters for ever and ever
> Amid burnt sands that reward not the giver.[1]

They had seen Him "wounded for our transgressions . . . bruised for our iniquities" (Isa. 53:5 KJV), chastised for our peace, and stricken that we might be healed, and their hearts had been bowed and broken by His great love. Henceforth they were His bond slaves, no longer free to come and go as they pleased but only as He willed, for the adamantine chains of love held them and the burning passion of love constrained them. Such bondage and service became to them the most perfect liberty. Their only joy was to do those things that were pleasing in His sight. Set at liberty to do this, their freedom was complete, for only they are free who are permitted to do always that which pleases them. Love slaves have no pleasure like that of serving their Master. This is their joy and their very "crown of rejoicing" (1 Thess. 2:19 KJV).

Love slaves are altogether at their Master's service. They are all eyes for their Master. They watch. They are all ears for their Master. They listen. Their minds are willing. Their hands are ready. Their feet are swift. To sit at the Master's feet and look into His loved face, listen to His voice and catch His words, run His errands, do His bidding, share His privations and sorrows, watch at His door, guard His honor, praise His name, defend His person, seek and promote His interests, and, if necessary, die for His dear sake—this is the joy of love slaves, and this they count as perfect freedom.

A fine man was placed on a slave block in an Egyptian slave market. His master was selling him. Men were bidding for him. A passing Englishman stopped, looked, listened, and began to bid. The slave saw him and knew that the Englishman was a world traveler. He thought that if the Englishman bought him, he would be taken from Egypt, far from friends and loved ones, and he would never see them anymore. So he cursed the Englishman, raving and swearing and tugging at his chain that he might reach and crush him. But the Englishman, unmoved, at last outbid all others, and the slave was sold to him.

He paid the price, received the papers that made the slave his property, and then handed them to the man.

"Take these papers; you are free," he said. "I bought you that I might give you your freedom."

The slave looked at his deliverer and his ravings ceased. Tears flooded his eyes, as, falling at the Englishman's feet and embracing his knees, he cried, "O sir, let me be your slave forever. Take me to the ends of the earth. Let me serve you till I die!"

Love had won his heart, and now love constrained him. And he felt there could be no joy like serving such a master.

We see many illustrations of this bondage of love in our daily lives. Surely it is the glory and joy of the true wife. She would rather suffer hardship and poverty in a Kansas sod house, with the husband she loves, than live in a palace surrounded by every luxury with any other.

> And on her lover's arm she leant,
> And round her waist she felt it fold,
> And far across the hills they went
> In that new world which is the old . . .
> And o'er the hills and far away
> Beyond their utmost purple rim,
> Beyond the night, across the day,
> Thro' all the world she followed him.[2]

This bondage of love is, at one and the same time, the slavery and the freedom of the true mother. Offer such a mother gold and honors and pleasure, and she will spurn them all for the sacred joy of serving and sacrificing for her child.

This also is the true freedom and service of the Christian. "My yoke is easy, and my burden is light," said Jesus (Matt. 11:30 KJV). His yoke is the yoke of love, and it is easy. Love makes it easy. His burden is the burden of love, and it is light. Love makes it light.

To the unregenerate soul the yoke looks intolerable, the burden unbearable. But to those who have entered into the secret of the Master, His yoke is the badge of freedom, and His burden gives wings to the soul.

This is holiness. It is wholeness of consecration and devotion. It is singleness of eye. It is perfect love that casts out fear (see 1 John 4:18). Love slaves do not fear the Master, for they joy in the Master's will. The slave of love says, "Not my will, but yours, be done" (Luke 22:42 ESV) and, "Though he slay me, yet will I trust in him" (Job 13:15 KJV). There can be no fear where there is such love.

This is heart purity accomplished by the expulsive power of a new and overmastering affection and purpose. Sin and selfishness are consumed in the hot fires of this great love.

This is religion made easy. This is God's kingdom come, and His will done, on earth as it is in heaven. For what more can the angels do than serve God with this unselfishness and passionate love?

The love slave is gentle and forbearing and kind to all the children of the household and to all the other slaves, for the sake of the Master. Are they not dear and valuable to the Master? Then they are dear and valuable to the love slave for the Master's sake. And such are ready to lay down their lives to serve them even as to serve the Master. Such was Paul's spirit when he wrote, "Even if I am to be poured out as a drink offering upon the sacrificial offering of your faith, I am glad and rejoice with you all" (Phil. 2:17 ESV). And so likewise was it beautiful Queen Esther's spirit when, in uttermost consecration for her people's salvation, she sent word to Mordecai, "I will go to the king, even though it is against the law. And if I perish, I perish" (Est. 4:16 NIV).

Love slaves care nothing for their own lives (see Acts 20:24), because they belong to the Master. They have no other interests than those of the Master, want no other, will have no other. They cannot be bribed by gold or honors. They would rather suffer and starve for the Master than feast at another's table. Like Ruth, they say, "Don't ask me to leave you and turn back. Wherever you go, I will go; wherever you live, I will live. Your people will be my people, and your God will be my God. Wherever you die, I will die, and there I will be buried. May the LORD punish me severely if I allow anything but death to separate us!" (Ruth 1:16–17 NLT).

Do you ask, "How shall I enter into this sweet and gentle and yet all-powerful bondage of love?" I answer, by your own choice and by God's revelation of Himself to your soul. If your love to Him now is a very poor and powerless thing, it is because you do not know Him, you do not draw near enough to see His beauty.

"My God, how beautiful Thou art" is the language of a soul that is learning to know Him. Then comes the realization:

> Thou hast stooped to ask of me,
> The love of my poor heart.[3]

To the people of this world He is not beautiful, for they have not sought to see Him. Let Him show Himself to you that you may fall in love with Him. Paul had seen His glory and been blinded by it. The other apostles had lived with Him and walked at His side. They loved Him because they knew Him so well.

For this reason they could make the great decision. Like Moses they chose "rather to suffer affliction with the people of God, than to enjoy the pleasures of sin for a season; esteeming the reproach of Christ greater riches than the treasures in Egypt" (Heb. 11:25–26 KJV). So you must choose. The choice must be complete, and it must be final. Then as a love slave you must wait upon the Master. If He is silent to you, watch. When He speaks to you, listen. What He says to you, do. His will is recorded in His Word. Search the Scriptures. Meditate therein day and night. Hide His Word in your heart. Be not forgetful. Take time to seek His face. Imagine a slave being too busy to wait on his master, to find out his wishes! Take time, find time, make time to seek the Lord, and He will be found by you. He will reveal Himself to your longing, loving soul, and you shall know the sweet compulsions of the slavery that is love.

> Higher than the highest heavens,
> Deeper than the deepest sea,
> Lord, Thy love at last has conquered;
> Grant me now my spirit's longing
> None of self, and all of Thee![4]

NOTES

1. Rose Terry, "Give! As the Morning That Flows Out of Heaven," *Poems* (Boston: Ticknor and Fields, 1861), n. p.

2. Alfred Lord Tennyson, "The Day-Dream," *The Complete Works of Alfred Tennyson, Poet Laureate* (New York: R. Worthington, 1879), 72–73.

3. Frederick W. Faber, "My God, How Wonderful Thou Art," 1849, public domain.

4. Theodore Monod, "Oh, the Bitter Shame and Sorrow," 1874, public domain.

A Man in Christ 2

"I knew a man in Christ," wrote Paul (2 Cor. 12:2 KJV). Imagine someone writing, "I knew a man in Bonaparte, in Buddha, in Caesar," and we shall see at once how striking, how startling is this expression. We should not only be startled, but also shocked to hear this said of anyone but Christ Jesus. But the Christian consciousness is not offended by hearing of "a man in Christ." It recognizes Christ as the home of the soul, its hiding place and shelter from the storm, its school, its fortress and defense from every foe. He is not simply the Babe of Bethlehem, the Carpenter of Nazareth, the first of the religious teachers of Palestine, and the victim of religious bigotry and Roman power. He is the Prince of Peace, the Mighty God, the Everlasting Father, in whose bosom we nestle and in whose favor we find peace and comfort and salvation.

Do you know any man or woman in Christ? How many people do you know who live in Him and walk in the unbroken fellowship that being "in Christ" must imply? Do you know twenty? Ten?

But let us not judge others. Paul was not doing so. He was very generous in his judgments of his brothers and sisters. He addressed his letters as follows: "Paul, an apostle of Jesus Christ by the will of God, to the saints which are at Ephesus, and to the faithful in Christ Jesus" (Eph. 1:1 KJV). "Paul and Timotheus, the servants of Jesus Christ, to all the saints in Christ Jesus which are at Philippi" (Phil. 1:1 KJV). "Paul, an apostle of Jesus Christ by the will of God . . . to the saints and faithful brethren in Christ which are at Colosse" (Col. 1:1–2).

Paul reckoned his brothers and sisters to be in Christ. But this man whom he knew "in Christ" was not one of them, but Paul himself. He was the man. There was no doubt about him being in Christ. He wrote with complete assurance.

Can you speak with such assurance? Do you know yourself to be in Christ? Or ever to have been in Christ? What a profound fellowship and union!

But listen to Paul further: "I was caught up to the third heaven fourteen years ago. Whether I was in my body or out of my body, I don't know—only God knows. Yes, only God knows whether I was in my body or outside my body. But I do know that I was caught up to paradise and heard things so astounding that they cannot be expressed in words, things no human is allowed to tell" (2 Cor. 12:2–4 NLT).

Did you ever have a moment, or an hour, in which you were lost in fellowship with the Lord, having no thought of time or space, in which experiences were wrought in you, emotions swept through you, purity and love and power and comfort and assurance were imparted to you, that you have never been able fully to explain or express in words, or which, possibly, you have felt to be too sacred to try to tell or describe?

Such was Paul's experience. He was the man to whom the words make reference. And many people who are in Christ—possibly most or all who are in Him—have had some such moment, long or short it may have been, but indescribably sweet, precious above gold or silver, and memorable above any and all other experiences of life.

Oh, how invaluable is such an experience to a soul, especially in a time of fierce temptation! It sweeps away forever the intellectual and moral and spiritual fogs and uncertainties that cloud the mind and heart. It fixes a person's theology. It settles for us the fact that we are living souls, morally and spiritually responsible to God. We feel the breath of eternity in us.

Wrapped in that wondrous fellowship we know there is a heaven, and to lose God, we know, would be hell. Henceforth to us, heaven and hell are realities as assured as light and darkness, as truth and falsehood, as right and wrong. This experience establishes the Godhead of Christ. We know that "Jesus is Lord," not by what we have learned from a teacher, from books and creeds, but by revelation, "by the Holy Spirit" (1 Cor. 12:3 NLT).

If in hours of depression and temptation, the Enemy of our souls should suggest a doubt as to these great truths, we can instantly rout our foe by recalling the intimate revelations of that sacred experience which it is not possible to utter.

There are two experiences mentioned by Paul in 2 Corinthians 12:2–4. One is abiding—the blessed but common everyday experience that is new every morning and fresh every evening, that the dust and toil of the day, and the stillness and slumber of the night, do not break or disturb; it is the very life of the Christian. The other is transitory, the experience of a moment, comparatively.

"In Christ" is the abiding experience. We are to live in Christ. Daily, hourly, momently we are to choose Him as our Master, walk with Him, look to Him, trust Him, obey Him, and draw from Him our strength, wisdom, courage, purity—every gift and grace needed for our soul's life. The supply of all our need is in Him. Our sap, our life, our leaf, and our fruit are from Him. Cut off from Him we wither, we die, but in Him we flourish, we bring forth abundant fruit, we have life forevermore.

"Caught up to paradise" is the transitory experience. It passes in an hour and may, possibly, never in this life be repeated, any more than was the burning bush experience of Moses repeated, or the "still small voice" experience of Elijah, or the Jabbok experience of Jacob, or the transfiguration experience of Jesus.

Those experiences were brief, but their effects, their revelations were for eternity. They were not abiding experiences, but windows opened through which earth glimpsed heaven. The memory of that vision was imperishable, though the vision passed. The veil was withdrawn, and for one awe-filled, rapturous moment, the eyes of the soul saw the face of God and the spirit of a human being had unutterable fellowship with its Father.

People who have had such an experience will be changed, will be different from their former selves, and different from all others who have had no such experience. Henceforth for them "to live is Christ"

(Phil. 1:21 KJV), and the great values of life are not material, financial, social, or political, but moral and spiritual.

One of the poets illustrates this from Lazarus, who was raised to newness of life after four days of death:

> Heaven opened to a soul while yet on earth,
> Earth forced on a soul's use while seeing heaven . . .
> He holds on firmly to some thread of life . . .
> The spiritual life around the earthly life:
> The law of that is known to him as this,
> His heart and brain move there, his feet stay here . . .
> And oft the man's soul springs into his face
> As if he saw again and heard again
> His sage that bade him "Rise," and he did rise . . .
> He knows
> God's secret, while he holds the thread of life.
> He will live, nay, it pleaseth him to live
> So long as God please, and just how God please.[1]

The march of armies and overthrow of empires meant little to that man whose eyes God had opened. He was diligent in his daily business, he loved everybody and everything, and for the rest he trusted God. This is the mark of the man or woman who has seen God, who has been caught up, if only for a brief moment, into that ineffable and paradisiacal fellowship.

Such will be blessed if they are not disobedient to the heavenly vision—if, like Mary, who treasured in her heart the things spoken of her baby, Jesus, they treasure up the sacred revelation given to them in the moment of vision!

We cannot command such moments. They come to us, come unexpectedly, but they never come except to the one who is in Christ, who day by day lives for Christ, seeks His face, meditates on His ways and Word, takes time to commune with Him, wrestles with Him in prayer, seeks to glorify Him by good words and works, and waits and longs for Him more than they who through tedious hours of weary nights wait and long for the morning.

Let no humble, earnest souls be discouraged because they do not constantly live in such rapturous fellowship. Paul did not remain in paradise. It was a brief experience and was followed by a troublesome thorn in the flesh. These glimpses of heaven, these rapt moments of fellowship, are given to confirm faith and fit the soul for the toil and plodding service of the love slaves of Jesus, who fight and labor to help Him in His vast travail to save a world of souls from sin, from the Devil's grip, and from hell.

The common, everyday, abiding experience is a lowly, patient, loving life in Christ. This may be ours unbrokenly, and it should be.

"Anyone who belongs to Christ has become a new person," wrote Paul (2 Cor. 5:17 NLT). That person breathes the atmosphere of heaven while plodding the dusty roads of earth. He or she diffuses peace, promotes joy, kindles love, quiets fear, comforts mourners, and heals the broken heart.

In such a person Christ sees "the travail of his soul" (Isa. 53:11 KJV) and is satisfied. In them the long, stern trial and discipline of Christ's incarnation and the bitter agony of His cross begin to bear their full, ripe fruit, and the Master delights in them, calms them with His love, and rejoices over them with joyful songs (see Zeph. 3:17). In them the earnest expectation of all creation, which awaits the manifestation of the sons and daughters of God (see Rom. 8:19–22), begins to be fulfilled, the long night of earth's shame and sorrow and sin is passing, and the dawning day of the reign of peace and righteousness is breaking.

I knew a father in Christ whose children said, "It is easy to be good when father is around," not because they feared him and must be good, but because goodness flourished in the sunshine of his Christlike presence.

I knew a husband in Christ whose wife said, "He is like David, who returned to bless his household." His presence was a benediction to his home.

I knew a man who had been a hard, brutal drunkard, but was now a blacksmith "in Christ." One day a farmer brought his mare to this blacksmith to have her shod, and with her he brought straps and tackle to strap her up, for she was so fearful or so savage that no one could shoe her otherwise. But the blacksmith "in Christ" said, "Let me get acquainted with her." He walked around her, stroked her gently, and spoke to her kindly and softly, while she rubbed her soft nose against him, smelled his garments, and got acquainted with him. She seemed to make a discovery that this was a new creature—a kind she had never met before, especially in a blacksmith's shop. Everything about him seemed to say to her, "Fear not," and she was not afraid. He lifted her foot and took off a shoe, and from that day forth he shod that mare without strap or tackle, while she stood in perfect quiet and unconcern.

Poor horse! She had waited all her lifetime to see one of the sons of God, and when she saw him she was not afraid.

And the whole earth is waiting for the unveiling, the manifestation, "the revelation of God's sons and daughters" (Rom. 8:19 CEB), waiting for the men and women, boys and girls, who live in Christ and in whom Christ lives. When the world is filled with such people or controlled by them, then—and only then—will strikes and wars, bitter rivalries and insane hatreds, and disgusting and hellish evils cease, and the promise and purpose of Christ's coming be fulfilled.

NOTE

1. Robert Browning, "An Epistle Containing the Strange Medical Experience of Karshish, the Arab Physician," *Poems of Robert Browning* (London: Oxford University Press, 1923), 119–120.

Future Punishment and the Bible 3

Joseph Cook, one of America's soundest and clearest thinkers, said to me a generation ago, "Let the churches banish from their pulpits the preaching of hell for a hundred years, and it will come back again, for the doctrine is in the Bible, and in the nature of things." And in his great lecture, "Final Permanence of Moral Character," he said, "The laws by which we attain supreme bliss are the laws by which we descend to supreme woe. In the ladder up and the ladder down in the universe, the rungs are in the same side-pieces. The self-propagating power of sin and the self-propagating power of holiness are one law. The law of judicial blindness is one with that by which the pure in heart see God."[1]

There is but one law that can save me from "the law of sin and death," and that is "the law of the Spirit of life in Christ Jesus" (Rom. 8:2 KJV). If I refuse to submit to that law, I abide eternally under the law of sin and death and endure eternally its dread penalties.

"Every sinner must be either pardoned or punished," I once heard The Salvation Army's founder say in the midst of an impassioned appeal to people to make their peace with God. They have remained in my memory, always representing a tremendous truth from which we can never get away.

The atonement opens wide the door of pardon, uttermost salvation, and bliss eternal to every penitent soul who will believe in Christ and follow Him, while it sweeps away every excuse from the impenitent heart that will not trust and obey Him. The atonement justifies God in all His ways with sinful men and women.

The holiest beings in the universe can never feel that God is indifferent to sin, when He pardons believing souls, lifts up their drooping heads, and introduces them to the glories and blessedness of heaven, because Christ has died for them. On the other hand, the souls who are lost and banished to outer darkness cannot blame God nor charge Him with indifference to their misery, since Christ, by tasting death for them, flung wide open the gateway of escape. That they definitely refused to enter in will be clear in their memory forever and will leave them without excuse.

We do not often encounter now the old-fashioned universalist, who believed that everyone, whether righteous or wicked, enters into a state of blessedness the moment they die. But others, with errors even more dangerous (because seemingly made agreeable to natural reason and to our inborn sense of justice) have come to weaken people's faith in the tremendous penalties of God's holy law. In fact, there seems to be a widespread and growing tendency to doubt the existence of hell and the endless punishment of the wicked.

A theory often advanced is the annihilation, or extermination, of the wicked. It is said that there is no eternal hell, and that the wicked do not enter into a state of punishment after death but are immediately or eventually blotted out of existence.

Then there is the doctrine of "eternal hope." This asserts that the wicked will be punished after death, possibly for ages, but that in the end they will all be restored to the favor of God and the bliss of the holy. The words of our Lord to the traitor appear to be an unanswerable refutation of this doctrine. If all are to be saved at last, would Jesus have said of Judas, "It would have been better for that man if he had not been born" (Mark 14:21 ESV)? For what are ages of suffering when compared to the blessedness and rapture of those who finally see God's face in peace and enjoy His favor to all eternity?

There is something so awful about the old doctrine of endless punishment, and such a seeming show of fairness about these new doctrines, that the latter appeal very strongly to the human heart and enlist on their behalf all the sympathies and powerful impulses of "the sinful nature [which] is always hostile to God" and which "never did obey God's laws, and . . . never will" (Rom. 8:7 NLT).

In forming our opinions on this subject we should stick to the Bible. All we know about the future state is what God has revealed and left on record in "the law and . . . the testimony" and "if they speak not according to this word, it is because there is no light in them" (Isa. 8:20 KJV). Human reason as well as human experience fails us here, and we can put no confidence in the so-called revelations of spiritualism nor in the dreams of sects who pretend to be able to probe the secrets of eternity. If the Bible does not settle the question for us, it cannot be settled.

The Bible teaches that there is punishment for the wicked after death, and that they are conscious of this punishment. In the record of the rich man and Lazarus, Jesus said, "The rich man also died and was buried, and his soul went to the place of the dead. There, in torment, he saw Abraham in the far distance with Lazarus at his side. The rich man shouted . . . 'Send Lazarus over here to dip the tip of his finger in water and cool my tongue. I am in anguish in these flames'" (Luke 16:22–24 NLT).

Some labor hard to strip this Scripture of its evident meaning and to rob it of its point and power by declaring that it is only a parable. On the contrary, the Savior's statements are given as facts. But even if we admit the account to be a parable, what then? A parable teaches either what is or what may be, and in that case these words lose none of their force but stand out as a bold word picture of the terrible doom of the wicked.

Over and over Jesus spoke of the wicked being cast into "outer darkness," where "there shall be weeping" and "wailing and gnashing of teeth" (Matt. 8:12; 13:42 KJV). Three times in one chapter He spoke of the worm that never dies and the fire that is not quenched (see Mark 9).

Paul said that "indignation and wrath, tribulation and anguish" (Rom. 2:8–9 KJV) shall come upon the wicked. And John said they are in torment (see Rev. 14:10–11).

What can all this mean but conscious punishment? Let those who never before saw the Bible read these words for the first time and they would at once declare that the Bible teaches the conscious suffering of the wicked after death. They might not believe the teaching, but they would never think of denying that such was the Bible's teaching.

The punishment mentioned in the Bible must be felt—it must be conscious—otherwise it is not "torment" and "tribulation and anguish."

The "second death," the death of the soul, must be something other than the destruction of its conscious existence.

Jesus has defined eternal life for us as the knowledge of God: "This is eternal life, that they know you the only true God, and Jesus Christ whom you have sent" (John 17:3 ESV). If then this blessed knowledge constitutes eternal life, what is the death which sin imposes but just the absence of this knowledge, with consequent wretchedness and misery? To lose God, to sink into outer darkness, to lose all fellowship with pure and loving souls, to be an outcast forever—this is "the second death," this is "torment and anguish," this is hell, and this is "the wages of sin" (Rom. 6:23 KJV).

The Bible further teaches that the punishment of the wicked after death will be endless. There are distinguished teachers and preachers who have declared that the Bible does not teach the eternity of sin and punishment. But if we examine for ourselves, we find this teaching as clear as human language can make it. We read: "Whoever blasphemes against the Holy Spirit never has forgiveness, but is guilty of an eternal sin" (Mark 3:29 ESV)—and eternal sin will surely be followed by eternal woe. While sin lasts, misery lasts.

The strongest terms that can be used have been used to teach eternal punishment. When we say a thing will last forever we have put it strongly, but when we duplicate the phrase and say it will last forever and forever, we cannot add to its strength—we have said all that can be said. This is just what the Bible does in speaking of the punishment of the wicked.

The phrase "forever and ever" is the strongest term by which the idea of eternity is expressed in the Bible. It is the phrase used to express the eternal life and glory of the righteous: "And they shall reign for ever and ever" (Rev. 22:5 KJV). Paul used these words when he prayed for the continuance of God's glory: "To whom be glory for ever and ever" (Gal. 1:5 KJV; see also Phil. 4:20; 2 Tim. 4:18; Heb. 13:21). It is also the very phrase used to assert the eternal existence of God Himself, "the one who lives forever and ever" (Rev. 4:9 NLT).

This phrase, which is used to declare the endless life and glory of the righteous and the existence of God Himself, is also used to declare the endless punishment of Satan: "The devil that deceived them was cast into the lake of fire and brimstone, where the beast and the false prophet are, and shall be tormented day and night for ever and ever" (Rev. 20:10 KJV). In Revelation 20:15, we are told that the wicked are to share the punishment of the Devil himself. And Jesus, in foretelling the sentence of the wicked at the judgment day, declared, "Then the King will turn to those on the left and say, 'Away with you, you cursed ones, into the eternal fire prepared for the devil and his demons'" (Matt. 25:41 NLT), thus showing that the wicked are to share the punishment of the Devil, which is "for ever and ever."

Did not Jesus mean to teach endless punishment when, three times in six short verses, He warned His hearers in the most solemn manner to cut off hands and feet and pluck out eyes rather than to go into hell, "where their worm does not die and the fire is not quenched" (Mark 9:43–48 ESV)?

Is not endless punishment implied in the parable of the cruel and unforgiving servant, who, owing an enormous debt with nothing with which to pay, was delivered to the tormentors till he should pay all that was due? Does not Jesus mean to teach that the man's debt was beyond his power to cancel and that, since he proved wickedly unworthy of mercy and forgiveness, he was buried forever beneath the burden and torment of his vast debt? And this parable simply pictures the moral and spiritual debt of the sinner—illimitable and ever-increasing, unless, in penitence and obedient faith, he finds release through the blood of Christ before the final sentence of judgment is passed and the prison gates have closed upon him.

We learn from the Jewish historian Josephus that the Jews believed in endless punishment. And when the Son of God came into the world to teach people the truth, He did not deny and combat that belief but spoke fearfully plain words that would confirm and strengthen it.

Well does one writer say, "They who deny that any of the words used of future punishment in Holy Scripture express eternity, would do well to consider whether there is any way in which Almighty God could have expressed it, which they would have accepted as meaning it."[2]

God did not trifle when He inspired those dreadful warnings. Take heed, then, that you do not trifle when you read them, but rather fear and tremble at the Word of the Lord. For just in proportion as you, in the secret of your own heart, doubt the endless punishment of the wicked, in that proportion you will lose the power to resist sin and the desire to save your own soul or those of others around you.

Two powerful motives the Holy Spirit uses to lead men and women to accept the Savior and renounce all sin are the hope of everlasting blessedness and the fear of eternal woe. In the heart of a Christian these motives may, in time, be swallowed up in a higher motive of love and loyalty to God, but they always remain as a framework. No preacher through all the ages has appealed so simply, constantly, powerfully, and with such even balance to these motives as did the Savior. The whole of Matthew 25 is an illustration of His method of appeal.

Eternity furnishes these motives. They balance each other like the two wings of a bird, the two wheels of a carriage—right and left, upper and lower, right and wrong—and this balance is never lost, but evenly held throughout the Bible from the blessing and cursing of Deuteronomy (see 30:19) to the final fixedness of moral character as "filthy" or "holy" in Revelation (22:11 ESV). Deny one of them and your strength against sin is gone. You may live a life most beautiful in its outward morality, but those secret girdings of the will which in the past impelled you to resist sin unto death will weaken, and you will find yourself making secret compromises with sin. You will lose your power to discern the exceeding sinfulness of sin (see Rom. 7:13 KJV). You will be ensnared by Satan masquerading as an angel of light, and someday you will become a servant of sin.

Sinners are not alarmed by the thought that death ends all. They will say, "Let us eat and drink, for tomorrow we die" (1 Cor. 15:32 ESV). It is not death they fear, but that which follows death. Nor do they care for punishment after death if they can only believe it will end sometime; they will still harden themselves in sin and mock God. But preach to them the faithful Word of God until the awful fact of endless punishment, set over against the endless blessedness of God's approval and favor, pierces their guilty consciences and takes possession of their souls, and they will go mournfully all their days until they find Jesus the Savior.

Such has always been the effect of the doctrine when proclaimed in power and pity and love with the fire-touched lips of holy men and women. But let people in their folly imagine themselves wiser and more pitiful and just than God, and so begin to tone down this doctrine, then conviction for sin ceases, the instantaneous and powerful conversion of souls is laughed at, the supernatural element in religion is called fanaticism, the Holy Spirit is forgotten, and the work of God comes to a standstill.

But some object that God is not just to punish souls forever for the sins they commit in the short period of a lifetime. And thus speaking, they think of certain acts of sin such as lying, cheating, swearing, murder, or committing adultery. But it is not for these sins that men and women are sent to hell. God has pardoned multitudes who were guilty of all these sins, and has taken them home to heaven. All who are sent to hell go by the weight and pull of their self-chosen evil and discordant nature and character, because they will not repent and turn from sin to God, but choose to remain filled with unbelief, which begets pride and self-will. Consequently they are out of harmony with—and are antagonistic to—God and all His humble, obedient servants. They will not come to Jesus, that they may be saved from sin and receive a new heart and life. They are dead in trespasses and sins, and they refuse the Life-Giver. Jesus said, "You refuse to come to me that you may have life" (John 5:40 ESV). Again He said, "This is the basis for judgment: The light came into the world, and people loved darkness more than the light" (John 3:19 CEB).

If sinners would come to Christ and receive the gracious, loving life He offers, and allow Him to rule over them, God would not impute their trespasses to them, but would forgive all their iniquities, and their sins would drop off as the autumn leaves from the trees in the field.

But so many will not come. They refuse the Savior. They will not hear His voice. They turn away from His words and remain indifferent to His entreaties. They laugh or mock at His warnings. They walk in disobedience and rebellion. They trample on His holy commandments. They choose darkness instead of light. They prefer sin to holiness, their own way to God's way. They resist the Holy Spirit. They neglect and reject Christ crucified for them—and for this they are punished.

All this stubborn resistance to God's invitations and purposes may be linked to a life of external correctness and even apparent religiousness. Not until all His judgments and warnings, His entreaties and dying love, have failed to lead them to repentance and acceptance of the Savior—and not until they have utterly refused the eternal blessedness of the holy—does God cease to strive with sinners and follow them with tender mercies.

By obstinate persistence in sin, men and women come to hate the thing that God loves and to love the thing that God hates. Thus they become as dead to God's will, to holiness and to His plans for them, as the child destroyed by smallpox or diphtheria is dead to the hopes and plans of his or her mourning father and mother. And as such parents in sorrow put away the pestilence-breeding body of their dead child, so God puts sinners, in their utter spiritual corruption, away from His holy presence "and from the glory of his power" (2 Thess. 1:9 KJV).

How could God more fully show His estimate of sin, together with His love and pity and longing desire to redeem souls, than by dying for sinful men and women?

God in Christ Jesus has done that. But sinners trample on Christ's blood, reject His infinite mercy, resist His infinite love, and so harden themselves; hence they deserve eternal punishment, which will follow sin as surely as night follows day.

Is sin only a mild infirmity that we need not fear and that will yield to gentle reproof? Was the Son of God only playing at being a Savior when He came down and died for us? Or is sin an awful crime against God and all His creatures that can be remitted only by the shedding of blood? Is it a crime for which human souls are responsible, and of which they ought to repent? Is it a crime that tends to perpetuate itself by hardening men and women in evil, and that culminates in eternal guilt when they finally resist the Holy Spirit and totally and forever turn from Jesus the crucified, rejecting Him as their Savior and Lord?

If sin is such a crime—and the Bible teaches that it is—then God, as moral governor of the universe, having provided a perfect way, and having done all He could to persuade everyone to turn from sin, is under obligation, if He meets only with determined resistance, to place sinners under sentence of punishment, to oppose them and put them away forevermore from His holy presence and from the society of holy men and women and angels, where they can no more breed moral and spiritual pestilence nor disturb the moral harmony of God's government and people. And when God does so my conscience takes God's part against my sensibilities, against my own soul, and against a guilty world, and pronounces Him just and holy.

We live in a stern universe where fire will not only bless us, but also burn us; where water will both refresh and drown us; where gravitation will either protect or destroy us. We must not look at things sentimentally. If we love God and serve Him, all things will work for our good. But if we despise or neglect Him, we shall find all things working for our eternal undoing and misery. God does not send people to hell who are fit for heaven. The standard of fitness is made plain in the Bible, and God's tender and pitying love has provided for every sinner pardon for past sins through the death of Jesus, and purity, power, and abundant help for the present and future through the gift of the Holy Spirit, so that there will be excuse for none. If one whom I love commits some terrible crime, violating all the righteous and gracious laws that safeguard society and consequently is cast into prison, my sorrow—if I myself am the right kind of a man—will spring not from the fact that he is in prison but rather from the fact that his character makes him unfit to be out of prison. And if he should go to hell, my sorrow would be due, not to the fact that he was in hell, but rather to the fact that he so neglected and despised infinite love and mercy that he was unfit for heaven. Such a person would possibly be more unhappy in heaven than in hell, just as someone who has terribly inflamed eyes is more unhappy in the light of broad day than in the darkness of midnight.

Finally, for someone to say, "I believe in heaven, but I do not believe in hell," is much the same as saying, "I believe in mountains, but not in valleys; in heights, but not in depths." We cannot have mountains without valleys. We cannot have heights without depths. And we cannot have moral and spiritual heights without the awful possibility of moral and spiritual depths—and the depths are always equal to the heights. The high mountains are set over against the deep seas, and so heaven is set over against hell.

Every road leads two ways. The road that leads from New York to Boston also leads from Boston to New York. A traveler can go either way. So it is with the roadway of life. The soul who chooses the things

God chooses, loves the things God loves, and hates the things God hates, and who, with obedient faith, takes up the cross and follows Jesus, will go to the heights of God's holiness and happiness and heaven. But the man or woman who goes the other way will land in the dark, bottomless abysses of hell. Everyone chooses his or her own way.

> Once to every man and nation comes the moment to decide,
> In the strife of truth with falsehood, for the good or evil side;
> Some great cause, God's new Messiah, offering each the
> bloom or blight,
> Parts the goats upon the left hand, and the sheep upon the right,
> And the choice goes by forever "twixt that darkness and that light."[3]

Joseph Cook closed his address entitled "The Certainties of Religion" at the Chicago Parliament of Religions with these words:

I bought a book full of the songs of aggressive, evangelical religion . . . and I found in that little volume words which may be bitter indeed when eaten, but which, when fully assimilated, will be sweet as honey. I summarize my whole scheme of religion in these words, which you may put on my tombstone:

> Choose I must, and soon must choose,
> Holiness, or heaven lose.
> While what heaven loves I hate,
> Shut for me is heaven's gate.

Endless sin means endless woe,

Into endless sin I go,

If my soul, from reason rent,

Takes from sin its final bent . . .

As the stream its channel grooves,

And within that channel moves,

So does habit's deepest tide

Groove its bed, and there abide.

Light obeyed increaseth Light;

Light resisted bringeth night.

Who shall give me will to choose,

If the love of Light I lose?

Speed, my soul; this instant yield;

Let the Light its scepter wield.

While thy God prolongeth grace,

Haste thee toward His holy face.[4]

NOTES

1. Joseph Cook, *Rev. Joseph Cook's Monday Lectures on Life and the Soul* (London: Ward, Lock, and Co., 1879), 126.

2. Frank Nutcombe Oxenham, *What Is the Truth as to Everlasting Punishment?* (New York: E. P. Dutton and Company, 1881), 114.

3. James Russell Lowell, "The Present Crisis," n. d., public domain.

4. Joseph Cook, "Strategic Certainties of Comparative Religion," ed. John Henry Barrows, *The World's Parliament of Religions: An Illustrated and Popular Story of the World's First Parliament of Religions*, vol. 1 (Chicago: The Parliament Publishing Company, 1893), 542–543.

I Counted . . . and I Count   4

The apostle Paul, in his young and fiery manhood, was on the way to Damascus, "breathing threats and murder against the disciples of the Lord" (Acts 9:1 ESV), when Jesus met him and won his heart, and from that day Paul counted all things loss for Christ. He made an unconditional surrender and found such loveliness and grace in Jesus that he lost his heart to Him and devoted his whole life to the Master. Long years afterward he wrote, "What things were gain to me, those I counted loss for Christ" (Phil. 3:7 KJV).

Youth is the time for the steps that shape all future life. The man or woman who does not make such a consecration in youth is not likely to make it at all. Age is prudent, cautious, and often timid and fearful. Youth is generous and hopeful, courageous, daring, and unentangled. Youth is not held back by prudence and caution. Youth sees visions and is prepared to make sacrifices to realize the vision—

to transform it into something substantial that can be touched, handled, and used.

But by and by, age approaches with its cares and infirmities, weariness and insomnia, and deferred hopes and unfulfilled ambitions. With age comes the temptation to slow down, compromise, draw back, or hold back part of the price (see Acts 5:2).

No doubt Paul was so tempted. But it is also certain that he met the temptation squarely and in the open, for he declared to the Philippians and to the ages, "I counted . . . and I count." He counted the cost in the past, and he continued to count the cost with that same passion and spirit. "I counted . . . [and] I count everything as loss because of the surpassing worth of knowing Christ Jesus my Lord. For his sake I have suffered the loss of all things and count them as rubbish, in order that I may gain Christ and be found in him" (Phil. 3:7–9 ESV). He obeyed the word of Jesus: "Remember what happened to Lot's wife!" (Luke 17:32 NLT). He had put his hand to the plow, and he never looked back.

It was here that wise King Solomon failed. In his youth he had visions, he was humble, he sought the Lord and walked in His way, he obtained promises and prospered. But in his age he went astray, his consecration failed, the vision was dimmed, the glory departed, and great and sad was his fall.

It was at this point that Ananias and Sapphira failed. They had given themselves to the Lord but later they conspired to hold back "part of the price" (Acts 5:2 KJV) and perished in their hypocritical falsehood. It was a withdrawal of this kind on the part of Demas that so hurt Paul's heart when he wrote, "Demas has deserted me because he loves the things of this life" (2 Tim. 4:10 NLT).

It is only a consecration like Paul's—unconditional, complete, and sustained to the end—that will satisfy the human soul, meet the infinite claims of Jesus, and answer the awful needs of a world weltering in pride and lust and covetousness and sin.

People sink to what is low, mean, and devilish, but they can never be satisfied with such things. We may be gratified with base matters, but we can be satisfied only by the highest. As Augustine said, "Thou madest us for Thyself, and our heart is restless, until it repose in Thee."[1]

William Booth, as a boy, might have sold himself to sinful pleasures and enjoyed them to the full, but he would not have been satisfied. He might have engaged in business and built up a fortune and rolled in wealth, but he would not have been satisfied. He might have entered the navy or army and become a great military leader and hero, or he might have plunged into politics and risen to the premiership and guided the destinies of the British Empire, but he would not have been so satisfied as he was in following Jesus to save the lost and "turn them to a pardoning God."[2] He, too, counted all things loss for Christ and continued to so count them to the end of his long and laborious life. It was only by such complete and sustained consecration that he could be satisfied with himself. The human soul demands this; it will not be trifled with nor put off with paltry excuses when we sit alone with our conscience, as someday we surely must.

> I sat alone with my conscience,
> In a place where time had ceased,
> And we talked of my former living

In the land where the years increased.
And I felt I should have to answer
The question it put to me,
And to face the question and answer
Throughout an eternity.

The ghosts of forgotten actions
Came floating before my sight,
And things that I thought were dead things
Were alive with a terrible might.
And the vision of all my past life
Was an awful thing to face,
Alone with my conscience sitting
In that solemnly silent place.[3]

It is only by such uttermost and sustained consecration that we can satisfy the imperious claims of Jesus—claims not of an arbitrary will, but of infinite love. He does not *compel* us to follow Him; He *invites* us to do so, with the understanding that if we choose to follow, we must gird ourselves for lifelong service and uttermost devotion and sacrifice. "There is no discharge in that war" (Eccl. 8:8 KJV). Jesus said, "If any of you wants to be my follower, you must turn from your selfish ways, take up your cross daily, and follow me" (Luke 9:23 NLT). He said:

Don't imagine that I came to bring peace to the earth! I came not to bring peace, but a sword. "I have come to set a man against his father, a daughter against her mother, and a daughter-in-law against her mother-in-law. Your enemies will be right in your own household!" If you love your father or mother more than you love me, you are not worthy of being mine; or if you love your son or daughter more than me, you are not worthy of being mine. If you refuse to take up your cross and follow me, you are not worthy of being mine. If you cling to your life, you will lose it; but if you give up your life for me, you will find it. (Matt. 10:34–39 NLT)

No power compels us to follow Jesus in this way, but we can follow Him no other way. We deceive ourselves if we think we can follow Him in any other spirit than those passages describe.

I may stand at a distance and admire Him, applaud Him, and protest that I am His and that I love Him, but I do not follow Him unless I take up my cross and bear it to the end.

This is His own standard for those who wish to serve Him. There are so-called Christians who think a mere formal recognition of Him while their hearts are set upon money-making or ambitions of their own is sufficient; but He demands soldiers willing to lose all for His cause on earth.

He is a Man of war as well as the Prince of Peace, and no world conqueror ever required of His followers such absolute heart loyalty as Jesus does. And He must require this, for He is the Way—and since there is no other way, we must follow Him or perish (see John 14:6). No one compels another to become an aviator, but once someone chooses to become an aviator, he or she must obey the laws of aviation, or fail.

Jesus is the Truth, and truth is utterly rigorous and imperious in its claims (see John 14:6). We cannot juggle with the truth of the multiplication table. We either follow it or we do not. There is no middle ground. Call it arbitrary if you will, get angry and vex your soul over it if you will, but the multiplication table changes not. It is truth, and you must adjust yourself to it. It cannot bend to you. So Jesus is the Truth—He changes not, and we must adjust ourselves to Him, consecrate ourselves utterly to Him, and abide in Him, or we are none of His.

Jesus is the Life, and life must not be trifled with lest it be lost (see John 14:6). It can be lost, and its loss is irreparable. So we can lose Jesus—and we shall lose Him if we prove unfaithful to Him, if after having put our hand to the plow we turn back.

Finally, it is only by an utter and sustained consecration that we can meet the needs of the world about us. "You are the salt of the earth," said Jesus (Matt. 5:13 NLT). Salt saves from corruption. True Christians alone save society from utter corruption. But if our consecration fails, we lose our savor, our saltiness, and society falls into rottenness.

Who can estimate the harm that is done to Christianity by half-hearted Christians? The world looks on at selfish, ignoble lives spent by those who claim to know Christ, and says, "We see nothing in it. These people are just like us." No one said that of Paul, for they saw always in him a man who felt that Christ was worth leaving the whole world to gain.

"You are the light of the world," said Jesus (Matt. 5:14 NLT). People would stumble and grope in unutterable darkness but for the light of the cross. Womanhood is despised, childhood is neglected, manhood is depraved, terrifying superstitions reign, horrible cruelties abound wherever Jesus is not known and followed. And men and women who, having come to Him and taken up their cross to follow Him, then turn back or fail in their consecration not only sin against God and wrong their own souls; they also commit a crime against humanity, against the children who are growing up and the generations yet unborn.

Soldiers must be faithful unto death, otherwise they will dishonor themselves and betray their country. Far more so must the Christian be true, for we are light-bearers of eternal things, and if that light goes out—if our consecration fails—we will stumble on the dark mountains and at last fall into a bottomless pit of outer darkness, and others will stumble and fall with us.

Paul did not fail. He never swerved in his onward course, never looked back. He rejoiced in his sufferings for Jesus' sake and for the sake of others. And oh, how glad he must have been, how his heart must have exulted at the end, when he cried out, "I have fought a good fight, I have finished my course, I have kept the faith: Henceforth there is laid up for me a crown of righteousness, which the Lord, the righteous judge, shall give me at that day" (2 Tim. 4:7–8 KJV).

Does all this seem hard? Well, that is because I have written about our side only and have said nothing about how the Lord will help and bless and comfort and inwardly strengthen you, if you are wholly His and continue so to the end. He who met Paul on the Damascus road will meet you and give you light. He who stood by Paul in prison and in shipwreck will stand by you. He will show you what He wants you to do and empower you to overcome every difficulty if you will say to Him, "Lord, what do You want me to do?"

And then, at the end of the way there is the crown of life, the unspeakable rapture of His presence and love, the reunion with loved ones gone before, the triumph over every foe, the holy and exalted fellowship with those who have been faithful throughout the ages. It will be worthwhile to see and be associated with all the numberless saints who have overcome, having "washed their robes, and made them white in the blood of the Lamb" (Rev. 7:14 KJV).

But what shame and remorse to be banished with the other crowd—of traitors and cowards, of proud, unclean, selfish, faithless ones! In order to avoid that lot, let us, like Paul, count and continue to count all things as loss for Christ.

NOTES

1. St. Augustine, *The Confessions of St. Augustine*, trans. Edward B. Pusey (New York: Collier Books, 1961), 11.

2. Charles Wesley, "Give Me the Faith Which Can Remove," 1749, public domain.

3. Charles William Stubbs, "I Sat Alone with My Conscience," n. d., public domain.

The Angels' Song of Peace 5

Heavenly beings always put the things of heaven first. Our Lord Jesus always placed the thought of unseen and eternal glory before the trifles of earth.

I have been much impressed with the order of the prayer Jesus gave His disciples. Before teaching them to ask for daily bread or the forgiveness of sins or deliverance from evil or protection in time of temptation, He taught them to pray that the Father's name should be hallowed, that the kingdom of God might come, and that His will might be done on earth as it is in heaven. He put heavenly things first. God was the center of His thought and desire, God's glory His chief concern, and that was what He taught His disciples.

What Jesus taught His disciples He practiced Himself, as we learn from His prayer in John 17. Alone, deserted, on the eve of the denial of Peter and the great betrayal, His thought was for the Father's glory.

He asked that while men put Him to utter shame, the Father would glorify Him, but only that He might in turn glorify the Father.

When the captain of God's host appeared to Joshua, his first and only word was not the outlining of an attack upon the enemy, but this: "Take off your sandals, for the place where you are standing is holy" (Josh. 5:15 NLT). He would impress Joshua with the importance of holy and heavenly things.

And so with the heavenly host which appeared over the plain of Bethlehem. The first note of their song was, "Glory to God in the highest." They put heavenly things first. God was foremost in their thought, then His glory. Afterward they sang, "on earth peace" and "good will toward men" (Luke 2:14 KJV).

The law and the gospel are but the law and the spirit of heaven projecting themselves into this world. They are introduced to men and women for their salvation, for their guidance, and for the direction of their lives, desires, and aspirations. All who seek to keep God's law and who embrace the gospel are introduced into the life and spirit of heaven and become citizens of heaven. As heavenly beings, therefore, they must put heavenly things first; they must live the life of heaven upon earth. In the light of these truths, the Christmas song of the angels, sung over the sleepy little town of Bethlehem, becomes a guide to us in these days. Our chief business is to give glory to God, to put Him first in our lives, to have a divine jealousy for His honor.

This spirit of seeking God's glory first will make us fight sin. We shall hate sin, because it robs God of His own—of His right and His glory in human beings. Those who have this spirit would rather die than commit sin because they love to honor God. God is supreme in their thought. God is first in their love. All their affections embrace God, and their hearts mourn, sob, and break—or wax hot with holy indignation— when they see God dishonored, rejected, and unloved.

This spirit will lead us out to warfare for God. Those who possess it cannot sit still while the Devil has his own way and while God is robbed and wronged. It leads them to go out and plead, exhort, command, and compel others to turn from their evil ways, to give up sin, to yield their hearts to God, and to love and serve Him.

This Spirit also leads us to meditate, to plan, to take counsel with our own hearts, and in every way possible to find out the best means by which we can win others over to God's side, save them from their sins for God's glory, and turn them into warriors for His army.

This spirit makes sacrifice a joy and service a delight. Everything we have is at God's disposal. We give our whole life for the glory of our Lord. We only wish that we had a thousand lives and could live a thousand years to fight God's battles. Oh, blessed are they who are so filled with this spirit of heaven that they put heavenly things first and sing on earth while the angels sing in heaven, "Glory to God in the highest!"

It is only in proportion as this spirit possesses people and takes possession of the earth that the second note of the Christmas song of the angels becomes possible: "Peace on earth and goodwill toward men."

We live in an age when the brotherhood of all is much spoken about, both in exhortation and in literature, but there can be no brotherhood where there is no fatherhood. Brothers and sisters must have a common father, and those who disown or neglect their father have not the spirit that will make it possible to live at peace with, or show good-will toward, each other. We shall have peace on earth and goodwill among people, and we shall have it universally, when everyone recognizes God's fatherhood and gives God the glory which is His due.

Oh, how peacefully men and women live together, and how they love one another when they get right with God! How a true revival settles old grudges and local quarrels and family disputes and other wranglings and strivings! Love to God will beget tender love toward each other—true love, love that is patient, longsuffering, forbearing, unsuspicious, and that leads to just and righteous dealings and to truth and reliability in word and action. These are essential to true peace and goodwill toward all.

The Bible declares that there is a good time coming when we will learn war no more, when we will be ashamed to attack one another in war, when war colleges will be done away with. May that day hasten! But it will hasten only as heavenly things are put first. We may talk about the brutalities of war, about the widows and orphans who mourn their beloved slain, about the soldiers and civilians who are shattered and torn by shot and shell, and about the utter waste of property. But it is only as holy men and women prevail over those who are unholy by winning the world to love God that the glad time foretold by the prophet will be brought about.

Solomon said, "Pride leads to conflict" (Prov. 13:10 NLT). At the heart of every quarrel, in the confusion of every brawl, and in the hate and fury of every war, pride will be found—pride of opinion, of wit or wisdom, of physical strength, of position, of reputation, or of power. Truly humble people never begin strife. They speak softly.

They are willing to make concessions. They are "swift to hear, slow to speak, slow to wrath" (James 1:19 KJV). They "seek peace, and pursue it" (Ps. 34:14 KJV). As far as possible, they "live in peace with everyone" (Rom. 12:18 NLT).

If such people do get mixed up in a contention, they may fight, but it is for the sake of righteous and ordered peace, and not from pride of self. They are peacemakers, not strife-makers. They follow peace with everyone, and they do this because their lives, desires, affections, ambitions, and activities are all guided and ruled by one glad, glorious purpose—the glory of God. That purpose consumes pride. Human pride and pomp look utterly contemptible to the one whose eye is focused on God's glory.

And this desire for God's glory makes them peacemakers. They love their fellows because they are dear to the heart of God. A tender feeling of sympathy, love, and brotherhood steals into their hearts, takes captive all their affections, fills them with love of God's will, banishes hatred, disarms suspicion, and establishes within them God's kingdom of "righteousness and peace and joy in the Holy Spirit" (Rom. 14:17 ESV).

It is this spirit that has made Salvation Army slum officers mightier than police officials in the dark alleys and fetid cellars and garrets of London and New York. It was this that gave William Penn and David Brainerd such heavenly influence with the native tribes of New Jersey and Pennsylvania, and that enabled John Gibson Paton to work such miracles of salvation in the southern islands of the Pacific Ocean.

Unless influenced by this spirit, the nations will go on building battleships, casting great guns, and inventing new technology for the destruction of lives. But let every humble lover of Jesus Christ catch the spirit and sing the Christmas song of the angels, assured that God is on the side of the men and women of peace who love Him, seek His glory, and have hearts which brim over with goodwill.

Our God is "the God of peace" (Rom. 16:20 NLT). Let us wait on Him in fervent prayer and faith for the fulfillment of the angels' song, and put away hate and suspicion and strife forever from our hearts, that, as far as it is up to us, His will may be done on earth as it is done in heaven. He has made the nations of one blood; may they become of one spirit! It is our mission to make them so.

How shall we do this? How can I, a poor, weak, shortsighted, single-handed man, help to fill the world with peace and goodwill?

In the first place, by keeping my own heart with all diligence and letting the peace of God rule in it. To this end, if anyone wrongs me, I must beware of harboring ill will toward him or her and of thinking how I can get even with that person. I must remember how much worse Jesus was treated and how He prayed for His enemies—for the men who were leading Him to death and mocking Him in His agony. I must be filled with His blessed, loving, meek, forgiving spirit. It is no sin to be tempted to be angry and revengeful, but it is a sin if I yield in my heart to this temptation.

I must also be a man of peace in my own family, community, and church. I must seek to soothe instead of irritate the people around me, remembering that "a soft answer turns away wrath, but a harsh word stirs up anger" (Prov. 15:1 ESV).

Most importantly, though I cannot enter into the councils of kings and queens and presidents, and in such high places work for peace among the nations, I can enter into my closet and pray for these leaders with their heavy burdens of care and perplexity and responsibility, asking God to guide and help them to rule the world in peace.

Indeed, we are exhorted to do this. Here is blessed and important knee-work for every humble follower of Jesus, in which he or she may mightily help to prevent war and maintain the peace of the world. Listen to Paul: "I urge you, first of all, to pray for all people. Ask God to help them; intercede on their behalf, and give thanks for them. Pray this way for kings and all who are in authority so that we can live peaceful and quiet lives marked by godliness and dignity" (1 Tim. 2:1–2 NLT).

God does not set us to pray in vain, and if we will pray in love and faith, we can help to establish the peace of the world. Let us exalt our calling to be people of peace, peacemakers, and let us pray with faith and great gladness, and God will hear and give us peace. And "when He gives quietness, who then can make trouble" (Job 34:29 NKJV)?

Misrepresenting God **6**

I read recently of a speaker who preached on the mercy of God "until it seemed there was nothing in God but mercy." But I fear he misrepresented God. Such misrepresentation is easy, and to people who do not think deeply, and who do not want to take life seriously, it is pleasant. But it is unspeakably dangerous.

If we are to win souls and save our own, we must not distort the picture of God's character that we hold up to view. It is life eternal to know God and Jesus Christ whom He has sent (see John 17:3), but it must be the true and holy God, as He is, and not some false god who conforms to our poor little warped human desires and opinions.

Some religious teachers misrepresent God by making Him utterly savage and cruel. They gloat over unutterably horrid pictures of hell, where they imagine God delighting in the most exquisite tortures of the damned, and thus people are embittered against God until they feel there is no hope of His mercy.

Others misrepresent God by making Him appear as a sort of goody-goody God, who fawns upon sinners with mawkish sympathy and looks upon worldly and trifling people and lukewarm Christians with weak, sentimental pity. Nothing can be further from the truth concerning God. We find God Himself bitterly rebuking those who, living in sin, thought He did not disapprove of their ways. He set before them a list of their sins (see Ps. 50:17–20), and then said, "While you did all this, I remained silent, and you thought I didn't care. But now I will rebuke you, listing all my charges against you. Repent, all of you who forget me, or I will tear you apart, and no one will help you" (Ps. 50:21–22 NLT).

The truth lies between these extremes. There is mercy in God, but it is mingled with severity; there is wrath in God, but it is tempered with mercy.

The great soul-winners from Bible times till now have recognized this. They have held an even balance between the goodness and the severity of God, because that is what the Bible does. And the Bible, of all the innumerable books written, is the only one that gives us an authoritative representation of God.

The book of nature reveals to us the goodness and the severity of God. Fire will not only bake our food and bless us, but it will also burn us. Water will not only quench our thirst and refresh us, but if we trifle with it, it will drown us. If we recognize God's ways of working in nature, and take heed and obey, we shall find nature's laws most kind and helpful. If we neglect or refuse to obey, we shall find them most terrible and destructive. But if we want to know God in all the richness of His character and all the fullness of His self-revelation, we must study the Bible and compare Scripture with Scripture.

The Bible tells us of God's unutterable love leading Him to seek sinners in mercy, but His righteousness requires penitence, faith, separation from evil, and obedience to His will.

Various Bible descriptions show how God holds an even balance between His mercy and His judgments. "Notice how God is both kind and severe," wrote Paul. "He is severe toward those who disobeyed, but kind to you if you continue to trust in his kindness. But"—showing that God's goodness does not destroy His severity, Paul said—"if you stop trusting, you also will be cut off." We must beware! Then he adds a touch of tenderness, making clear how even in His severity God waits to show mercy: "And if the people of Israel turn from their unbelief, they will be grafted in again, for God has the power to graft them back into the tree" (Rom. 11:22–23 NLT).

Again Paul wrote: "For I am not ashamed of this Good News about Christ. It is the power of God at work, saving everyone who believes. . . . This Good News tells us how God makes us right in His sight. This is accomplished from start to finish by faith. As the Scriptures say, 'It is through faith that a righteous person has life'" (Rom. 1:16–17 NLT). And then he adds, "But God shows his anger from heaven against all sinful, wicked people who suppress the truth by their wickedness" (Rom. 1:18 NLT).

And again he wrote:

Don't you see how wonderfully kind, tolerant, and patient God is with you? Does this mean nothing to you? Can't you see that his kindness is intended to turn you from your sin?

But because you are stubborn and refuse to turn from your sin, you are storing up terrible punishment for yourself. For a day of anger is coming, when God's righteous judgment will be revealed. He will judge everyone according to what they have done. He will give eternal life to those who keep on doing good, seeking after the glory and honor and immortality that God offers. But he will pour out his anger and wrath on those who live for themselves, who refuse to obey the truth and instead live lives of wickedness. There will be trouble and calamity for everyone who keeps on doing what is evil. . . . But there will be glory and honor and peace from God for all who do good—for the Jew first and also for the Gentile. For God does not show favoritism. (Rom. 2:4–11 NLT)

The saving mercy of God revealed in the Scriptures is invariably set over against the wrath of God, as the great mountains are set over against the deep seas. The writer to the Hebrews said of Jesus, "He is also able to save to the uttermost those who come to God through Him" (Heb. 7:25 NKJV), while Paul wrote of some upon whom "wrath has come . . . to the uttermost" (1 Thess. 2:16 NKJV).

There is, then, an uttermost salvation for all who "trust and obey" and an uttermost woe for all who go on in selfish unbelief and worldliness and sin. Truly "God is not mocked" (Gal. 6:7 KJV), and He is a God of judgment.

We find Jesus kept this balance when He said that those who hear His sayings and do them are like those who build upon a rock, against which rain and floods and winds cannot prevail, while those who hear and do not obey are like those who build upon sand, which will be swept away by rain and floods and wind (see Matt. 7:24–27). He also said that the wicked shall "go away into everlasting punishment: but the righteous into life eternal" (Matt. 25:46 KJV). He told of the shut door at the marriage, with some on the inside with their Lord and some on the outside, rejected and unknown; of the joy of the Lord into which good and faithful servants enter, and the outer darkness, into which the wicked and slothful are cast; and of the great, fixed gulf which is impassable, with some on the right side in the bosom of comfort and security and peace, and some on the wrong side in the bitter woe of fierce remorse and torment.

We find John the Baptist was faithful to this great truth. He cried out, "Anyone who believes in God's Son has eternal life. Anyone who doesn't obey the Son will never experience eternal life but remains under God's angry judgment" (John 3:36 NLT).

Likewise all through the Old Testament this balance is maintained:

Wash yourselves and be clean! Get your sins out of my sight. Give up your evil ways. Learn to do good. Seek justice. Help the oppressed. Defend the cause of orphans. Fight for the rights of widows. "Come now, let's settle this," says the LORD. "Though your sins are like scarlet, I will make them as white as snow. Though they are red like crimson, I will make them as white as wool. If you will only obey me, you will have plenty to eat. But [and here is the unfailing alternative] if you turn away and refuse to listen, you will be devoured by the sword of your enemies." (Isa. 1:16–20 NLT)

These Bible word pictures show us that no single word—not even the sweet word *mercy*—will sum up the rich and manifold character of God. The Bible says, "God is love" (1 John 4:8 KJV), but it also says, "Our God is a consuming fire" (Heb. 12:29 KJV).

To penitent hearts who trust in Jesus, God will be found to be rich in mercy. But He will defend the moral and spiritual order of His universe by uttermost penalties against those who go on proudly, carelessly, or wickedly in their own ways.

When Dr. Samuel Johnson lay dying, he was much concerned about his soul. A friend said to him, "Sir, you seem to forget the merits of the Redeemer."

"No," replied Dr. Johnson, "I do not forget the merits of the Redeemer, but I remember that He said He would place some on His right hand and some on His left."

Our only hope is in the wounds of Jesus and the shelter of His blood. There, and only there, shall we find mercy, since we have sinned. But there mercy is boundless and free.

Confessing Other People's Sins 7

"Have you eaten from the tree whose fruit I commanded you not to eat?" (Gen. 3:11 NLT), the Lord asked Adam in the garden of Eden. "The man replied, 'It was the woman you gave me who gave me the fruit, and I ate it.' Then the LORD God asked the woman, 'What have you done?' 'The serpent deceived me,' she replied. 'That's why I ate it'" (Gen. 3:12–13 NLT).

They confessed the sins of others and ignored their own, and the curse fell upon them instead of blessing. Nothing more surely makes manifest a person's spiritual blindness and hardness of heart than hiding behind others and confessing their faults instead of his or her own. It is a deadly kind of hypocrisy. It can meet only with God's displeasure.

"People who conceal their sins will not prosper," said Solomon, "but if they confess and turn from them, they will receive mercy" (Prov. 28:13 NLT). There is no more dangerous way of trying to cover one's sins than by blaming others and calling attention to their faults instead of humbly confessing our own.

An incident in the life of King Saul makes this plain:

> One day Samuel said to Saul . . . "This is what the LORD of Heaven's Armies has declared: I have decided to settle accounts with the nation of Amalek. . . . Now go and completely destroy the entire Amalekite nation—men, women, children, babies, cattle, sheep, goats, camels, and donkeys." . . .
>
> [But] Saul and his men spared Agag's life and kept the best of the sheep and goats, the cattle, the fat calves, and the lambs— everything, in fact, that appealed to them. They destroyed only what was worthless or of poor quality.
>
> Then the LORD said to Samuel, "I am sorry that I ever made Saul king, for he has not been loyal to me and has refused to obey my command." . . .
>
> When Samuel finally found him, Saul greeted him cheerfully. "May the LORD bless you," he said. "I have carried out the LORD's command!"
>
> "Then what is all the bleating of sheep and goats and the lowing of cattle I hear?" Samuel demanded.
>
> "It's true that the army spared the best of the sheep, goats, and cattle," Saul admitted. "But they are going to sacrifice them to the LORD your God. We have destroyed everything else." (1 Sam. 15:1–3, 9–11, 13–15 NLT)

Saul tried to cover his own sin by confessing the sins of others. But Samuel answered him, "Because you have rejected the command of the LORD, he has rejected you as king" (1 Sam. 15:23 NLT). So Saul lost his kingdom.

And people still lose their crown of peace and salvation and God's favor by sinning, by disobeying, and by confessing the sins of others instead of their own.

"Confess your sins to each other," wrote James (5:16 NLT). "If we confess our sins to him, he is faithful and just to forgive us our sins and to cleanse us from all wickedness," wrote John (1 John 1:9 NLT).

"I have sinned," cried David (2 Sam. 12:13 NLT). Again, he said, "I recognize my rebellion; it haunts me day and night" (Ps. 51:3 NLT). We can hear the sob of a broken and penitent heart through the open and humble confession. And God put away his sin.

"God, be merciful to me, for I am a sinner," prayed the tax collector, and Jesus said he "returned home justified before God" (Luke 18:13–14 NLT).

"Are you saved?" I asked a woman in one of our prayer meetings.

"No, I am not," she replied with emphasis.

"Were you ever saved?" I asked.

"Yes, I was."

"And what did Jesus do that you turned your back on Him and started for hell?" I questioned.

"A man who called himself a Christian slapped my husband in the face," said she—but she did not tell me the fact (which I learned later) that the man confessed his wrong and apologized.

"Well, that was too bad," I replied. "But you shouldn't have turned your back on Jesus for that. You know they slapped Jesus in the face, they 'smote him with the palms of their hands'" (Matt. 26:67 KJV).

And she opened her eyes wide and looked at me.

"And you know they spat in His face also, and not content with that, they crushed a crown of thorns on His head. But that did not satisfy them, so they bared His back, and tied His hands to His feet, and whipped His poor bare back till it was all cut and torn and bleeding. That was the way the Roman soldiers, under Pilate, scourged Him. And then they smote Him on the head and mocked Him. But not content with that, they then placed a great cross on His shoulders, and it must have pressed heavily upon the poor, wounded back. But He carried it, and there on Calvary they crucified Him. They drove great nails through His hands and feet, and lifting the cross they let it fall heavily into its place. This must have rent and torn His hands and feet very terribly, but He prayed, 'Father, forgive them.' And there He hung in agony and pain, while they robbed Him of His only suit of clothes, gave Him gall and vinegar to drink, and wagged their heads and mocked Him. Then He bowed His head and died. And this He suffered for you, my sister, but you turned your back upon Him because someone ill-treated your husband!"

And as I talked she saw Jesus. The sin of the other man faded from her sight and her own sin grew big before her eyes, until she was in tears. Then, rising, she rushed, sobbing, to the penitent form (the place to kneel for confession) to confess her own sin to the Lord and, I trust, to be restored once more to His favor.

When we get this vision of Jesus, we cease to blame others and look only at our own sin, which we can no longer excuse. We blame ourselves, plead guilty, and confess our wrongdoing with a broken and contrite heart. Then, looking into the pitying face of our suffering Savior, we trust, receive pardon, enter into peace, and become new creatures in Christ Jesus.

This is the vision and faith that begets love for the Savior, that produces obedience in the heart, that saves from all sin, and that gives love and skill to save others also.

Let me beg you to take your eyes off other people and fix them upon yourself and upon Jesus. Then you will "get rid of the log in your own eye . . . [and] you will see well enough to deal with the speck in your friend's eye" (Matt. 7:5 NLT).

And you who have to deal with people who are always confessing other people's sins, let me beg of you to deal with them tenderly, though firmly, lest you forget "the hole of the pit from which *you* were dug" (Isa. 51:1 NKJV, emphasis added) and lest you become severe with your brother or sister for a fault from which you may think yourself delivered, but are not entirely free.

Remember Paul's words: "Brothers and sisters, if another believer is overcome by some sin, you who are godly should gently and humbly help that person back onto the right path. And be careful not to fall into the same temptation yourself" (Gal. 6:1 NLT). I have seen people fall themselves through failing to be gentle with those who have fallen. Remember the words of Jesus: "Learn from me, for I am gentle and humble in heart" (Matt. 11:29 NIV). How hard is that sweet lesson of meekness and lowliness of heart! But that is the first lesson Jesus sets us to learn.

The Dangers of Middle Age 8

We read and hear much about the dangers of youth, and they are very many and often very deadly. But how little do we hear about the dangers of the middle-aged! And yet they, too, are very many and very deadly.

I was reminded vividly of this recently when a man, considerably past fifty years of age, stopped me on the street and sought an interview. After a rather close examination, in which I sought to locate and diagnose his spiritual disease, he told me of his sins and temptations. He had been a follower of Jesus but had fallen. He was becoming more and more entangled in a network of evil and was sinking deeper and deeper in the quicksand of his iniquity—and his sins were sins of the flesh!

The middle-aged are not altogether safe from the awful corruption and blasting sin which lies lurking in the lusts of the flesh. Joseph, when but a young man in Egypt, fully and grandly overcame this danger; he kept himself pure and set an example for the ages. But in middle life David and his son, Solomon, with all their light and wisdom, fell grievously and wallowed in sin and shame, thus bringing reproach upon God's people and God's cause, stirring up the enemies of the Lord to mock and blaspheme, and, doubtless, encouraging others by their example to fall into like sins.

But we do not have to go back to ancient history nor to the ranks of those who make no profession of religion to find how sins of the flesh overthrow middle-aged men and women if they do not watch and pray and walk softly with the Lord. I shall never forget the shock and chill that went through the hearts of American Christians some years ago, when a silver-haired evangelist—the author of a number of books of great spiritual insight and power, and one of the mightiest preachers it has ever been my lot to hear—fell into sin and shame. It was heartbreaking for his influence to be ruined, his good name spoiled, his reputation gone, his family put to shame, God's cause mocked, and for a soul whom he should have shepherded to be dragged to the mouth of hell to gratify his passing pleasure.

And there are a number of others I have known, who had great opportunities of usefulness, whose influence was widespread, and who walked in a broad day of spiritual light but who sank into a dark night of corruption, sin, and shame.

So let not only young men and women but mature ones as well take heed lest they fall. Let them watch for and guard themselves against the beginnings of sin—the unclean thought, the lascivious look, the impure imagination, the unholy desire. Let them hate "even the garment stained by the flesh" (Jude 23 ESV).

Let them beware of selling—for a mess of pottage—their good name, their sphere of usefulness, their place among God's people, the friendships of years, the honor of their children, the happiness of their home, the smile and favor of God, and their hope of heaven. Let them do as the writer to the Hebrews said: "Watch out that no poisonous root of bitterness grows up to trouble you, corrupting many. Make sure that no one is immoral or godless like Esau, who traded his birthright as the firstborn son for a single meal" (Heb. 12:15–16 NLT).

But the more constant spiritual danger of the middle-aged is the loss of the freshness of their early experience, the dew of their spiritual morning, the "devotion of [their] youth," when they were "holy to the LORD" and followed Him "in the wilderness" (Jer. 2:2–3 ESV).

There is nothing in the world so wonderful, beautiful, and delightful as the constant renewal of spiritual youth in the midst of the increasing cares, burdens, infirmities, losses, and disappointments of middle life and old age. And there is nothing so sad as the gradual loss of fervor, simplicity, heart devotion, unfeigned faith, triumphing hope, and glowing love of spiritual youth.

The psalmist called upon his soul to bless the Lord, who satisfied his mouth with good things, so that his youth—his soul's youth—was renewed like the eagle's (see Ps. 103:1–5).

But multitudes, instead of being renewed, fall into decay. They lose the bloom and blessedness of their early experience and become like Ephraim, of whom the prophet said, "Strangers devour his strength, and he knows it not; gray hairs are sprinkled upon him, and he knows it not" (Hos. 7:9 ESV). This loss may steal upon us like a creeping paralysis if we do not watch and pray.

It may come through a widening experience of human weakness and fickleness. We are continually tempted to lean upon human strength and ingenuity rather than upon God and His Word. And when others fail and fall we feel as though the foundations were swept away. At such times the Tempter will whisper, twisting God's Word: "What is the use of your trying to live a holy life? 'There is none who does good, not even one'" (Ps. 14:3 ESV). Then if we do not at once flee to and hide ourselves in Jesus, and lift our eyes to God, and stir up our faith toward Him, a chill of discouragement and doubt and fear will sweep over us; lukewarmness will take the place of the warm, throbbing experience of youth; and a half-skeptical, half-cynical spirit will fill the heart that once overflowed with glad, simple faith and abounding hope. It is this loss that often makes older folks look so coldly upon the return of those who have fallen, and that so unfits them to help and encourage those who are young in the faith.

Nothing filled me with greater admiration for The Salvation Army's founder than his morning-like freshness, his perennial youth, his springing hope, and his unfailing faith in God and humanity—in spite of all the shameful failures and desertions and backslidings which wounded him to the heart and pierced him through with many sorrows. And where he led shall we not follow?

Instead of looking at those who have fallen, why not look at those who have stood? Instead of losing heart and faith because of those who have thrown down the sword and fled from the field, shall we not shout for joy and emulate those who were faithful unto death, who came up out of great tribulation with robes washed in the blood of the Lamb? Why not shout for joy, and triumph with Joseph in his victory rather than sneer and lose faith in God and thus suffer defeat with David in his fall? Why not look at the beloved John and rejoice, rather than at the traitor Judas and despair? Why not consider Jesus, "who endured from sinners such hostility against himself"? If we do, we shall not "grow weary or fainthearted" (Heb. 12:3 ESV).

This loss may come through thronging cares and responsibilities. Youth and old age are largely free from responsibility, which comes pressing hard and insistently upon the middle-aged. There are business cares, family cares, and responsibility for church, city, and state. The wide-open, hungry mouths of the children must be fed; their restless, destructive feet must be shod; their health must be guarded; their tempers and dispositions must be corrected and disciplined; their eager, wayward, unformed minds must be trained and educated; and their souls must be found and saved.

And all these cares, which swarm about like bees, must be met again and again, and often when we are worn and weary and full of pain. No wonder that when Jesus spoke the parable of the sower, He mentioned the cares of life as among the weeds which choke the Word and make it unfruitful (see Luke 8:4–15). But no true follower of Jesus will run away from these cares. There is victory for those who are determined to have victory.

Moses was thronged with the care of a vast, untrained, stiff-necked, hungry multitude in a barren wilderness. But he walked with God, wore a shining face, and—with but one brief loss of patience, for which he duly suffered—he got victory, and God and angels conducted his funeral.

Daniel superintended a huge empire, with 120 provinces, but he found time to pray and give thanks three times a day, and was more than a conqueror.

Paul, in addition to whippings, stonings, imprisonments, shipwrecks, perils, hunger, cold, and nakedness, had pressing upon him
"the care of all the churches" (2 Cor. 11:28 KJV). But he rejoiced and
prayed and gave thanks, and did not murmur, faint, or turn back, and
God made him to triumph.

A distinguished writer has beautifully said:

Comradeship with God is the secret, not only of joy and peace,
but of efficiency. In that comradeship we find rest, not from
our work, but in our work. When Christ says, "Come unto me,
all ye that labour and are heavy laden, and I will give you rest.
Take my yoke upon you, and learn of me" [Matt. 11:28–29
KJV], He does not invite us to lay aside our work. He offers us
rest in our work. The invitation is to those who are laboring and
bearing burdens. The promise is to teach them how so to labor
and how so to bear their burdens so as not to be wearied by
them. It is not a couch which He offers us, but a yoke; and a
yoke is an instrument for the accomplishment of work.

For a yoke is not only an implement of industry; it is a
symbol of comradeship. The yoke binds two together. To take
Christ's yoke upon us is to be yoked to Christ. Work with Me,
says Christ, and your work will be easy; work with Me, and
your burden will be light.[1]

And this comradeship with the Lord Jesus is the secret of victory all
along the way and over every obstacle and every foe. Here—though
you may be tempted and tried, and almost overcome at the noon of

life—in fellowship with Jesus, the flesh loses its subtle power, the charms of the world are discovered to be but painted mockery, the Devil is outwitted, and while life is a warfare it is also a victory.

NOTE

1. Lyman Abbott, *Inspiration for Daily Living: Selections from the Writings of Lyman Abbott* (Boston: The Pilgrim Press, 1919), 329.

Maintaining the Holiness Standard   9

The Salvation Army was born not in a cloister or drawing room but on a spiritual battlefield—at the penitent form (the place at the altar for seeking forgiveness). It has been nourished for spiritual conquests not upon speculative doctrines and fine-spun verbal distinctions but upon those great doctrines which can be wrought into and worked out in soul-satisfying experience. Hence, The Salvation Army compels the attention of all men and women everywhere and appeals to the universal heart of humanity.

In this it is in harmony with the scientific spirit and practice of the age, which refuses to be committed to any theory that cannot be supported by facts.

One of The Salvation Army's central doctrines—and most valued and precious experiences—is that of heart holiness. The bridge The Salvation Army throws across the impassable gulf that separates the sinner from the Savior—who pardons that He may purify, who saves that He may sanctify—rests upon these two abutments: the forgiveness of sins through simple, penitent, obedient faith in a crucified Redeemer, and the purifying of the heart and empowering of the soul through the anointing of the Holy Spirit, given by its risen and ascended Lord, and received not by works, but by faith.

Remove either of these abutments and the bridge falls. Preserve them in strength, and a world of lost and despairing sinners can be confidently invited and urged to come and be gloriously saved.

The first abutment is deep grounded on such assurances as these: "With you there is forgiveness, so that we can, with reverence, serve you" (Ps. 130:4 NIV) and, "If we confess our sins, he is faithful and just to forgive us our sins, and to cleanse us from all unrighteousness" (1 John 1:9 KJV).

The second firmly rests on such Scriptures as these: "God knows people's hearts, and he confirmed that he accepts Gentiles by giving them the Holy Spirit, just as he did to us. He made no distinction between us and them, for he cleansed their hearts through faith" (Acts 15:8–9 NLT) and, "If we are living in the light, as God is in the light, then we have fellowship with each other, and the blood of Jesus, his Son, cleanses us from all sin" (1 John 1:7 NLT).

Such is the doctrine passed on to us from the first Christians, and here are some Scriptures which show how the doctrine was wrought into triumphant experience in their day:

> Don't you realize that those who do wrong will not inherit the Kingdom of God? Don't fool yourselves. Those who indulge in

sexual sin, or who worship idols, or commit adultery, or are male prostitutes, or practice homosexuality, or are thieves, or greedy people, or drunkards, or are abusive, or cheat people—none of these will inherit the Kingdom of God. Some of you were once like that. But you were cleansed; you were made holy; you were made right with God by calling on the name of the Lord Jesus Christ and by the Spirit of our God. (1 Cor. 6:9–11 NLT)

"Once we, too, were foolish and disobedient. We were misled and became slaves to many lusts and pleasures. Our lives were full of evil and envy, and we hated each other. But—when God our Savior revealed his kindness and love, he saved us, not because of the righteous things we had done, but because of his mercy. He washed away our sins, giving us a new birth and new life through the Holy Spirit. He generously poured out the Spirit upon us through Jesus Christ our Savior" (Titus 3:3–6 NLT).

Such was the doctrine of the first Christians, and such was their experience. And to this doctrine and experience The Salvation Army has been committed from the beginning. This has been both its reproach and its glory, and one of the chief secrets of its world-conquering power.

Some years ago, The Salvation Army's founder, William Booth, was in New York, and for nearly a week he stood before the thronging multitudes by night and before his own people by day, pleading for righteousness, for holiness, for God. As he toiled with flaming passion to accomplish his purpose, the great commandment began to unfold to me in fuller, richer meaning than ever before—"You shall love the

Lord your God with all your heart and with all your soul and with all your mind and with all your strength" (Mark 12:30 ESV). As he poured out his heart, I said to myself, "There is a man who loves God with all his heart."

Then, as I considered how his whole life was being poured without stint into God's service, I said, "There is a man who loves God with all his soul."

Again, when I noted how diligently and with what infinite study and pains he labored to make plain the great thoughts of God to the feeblest intellect, to the most darkened and degraded, to the least intelligent of his hearers, I said, "There is a man who loves God with all his mind."

And when I saw him old and worn, snowy white, and burdened with the weight of many years — with the heavy load of a world organization ceaselessly pressing hard upon him, still toiling, praying, singing, exhorting, into the late hours of the night, that Jesus might triumph and sinners be won — when it seemed that he ought to be seeking rest in sleep or retiring from the fight to the quiet and comfort of a pleasant home, yet joyously pressing on, I said, "There is a man who loves God with all his strength."

Afflicted, often wounded and heart-sore, burdened with care, he still seemed to me to fulfill each part of that great fourfold commandment. And that was holiness in action.

And it is this holiness — the doctrine, the experience, the action — that we Salvationists must maintain, or we shall betray our trust, lose our birthright, and cease to be a spiritual power in the earth. We shall have a name to live, and yet be dead; our glory will depart; and we, like Samson shorn of his locks, shall become as weak as others, and the souls with whom we are entrusted will grope in darkness or go elsewhere for soul nourishment and guidance. And while we may still have titles and ranks to bestow upon our children, we shall have no heritage to bequeath them of martyr-like sacrifice, spiritual power, daredevil faith, pure and deep joy, burning love, and holy triumph.

In this matter an immeasurable debt is laid upon us. We owe it to our Lord, who redeemed us by His blood not simply that the penalty of our sins should be remitted and that we should thereby escape the just deserts of our manifold transgressions, but also that we should be sanctified, made holy—that we should become temples of the Holy Spirit and live henceforth not for our own profit or pleasure, but for His glory, as His bondservants and friends, ready for service or sacrifice, and prepared for every good work.

We owe a great debt to the cloud of witnesses—the saintly souls who have gone before us. How shall we meet them without confusion and shame if we neglect or waste the heritage they have left us, which they secured for us with infinite pains, tears, prayers, wearisome toil, and often agony and blood? What a debt we owe to them!

We owe it to our children and our children's children. They look to us for the teaching that will direct them into full salvation. They will narrowly and constantly scan our lives to find in us an example of its fullness and beauty, its richness and power, its simplicity, its humility, its self-denial, its courage, its purity and unfailing constancy and steadfast trust, its goodness and meekness, its long-suffering love, its peace and joy, its patience and hope, and its deep and abiding satisfaction. How careful we should be not to fail or disappoint them!

We must pay this righteous debt. And we will. We must and will maintain our holiness standard in both our teaching and our experience, and in so doing we shall save both ourselves and them that hear us—those entrusted to us. This will be our glory and our joy.

But how shall we do this? It is not a simple or easy task. It may require the courage and devotion of a martyr. It will surely require the vigilance, prayerfulness, wisdom, and faithfulness of a saint.

We must remember that the standard is not man-made, but is revealed from heaven, and that those who experience the fullness of blessing still carry the treasure in earthen vessels. So while we should follow them as they follow Christ, we must not look to them but to Him and to His Word for the perfect and unchangeable standard of holiness.

Those who enter into this experience and abide in it are great students and lovers and seekers of God's Word, and to it they appeal when opponents arise.

Catherine Booth, the cofounder of The Salvation Army, read the Bible through eight times before she was twelve years old. Wesley said of himself, "I am a man of one book." Finney said:

I never pretend to make but one book my study. I read them occasionally, but have little time or inclination to read other books much while I have so much to learn of my Bible. I find it like a deep mine, the more I work it, the richer it grows. We must read that more than any or all other books. We must pause and pray over it, verse by verse, and compare part with part, dwell on it, digest it, and get it into our minds till we feel that the Spirit of God has filled us with the spirit of holiness. . . . I have often been asked by young converts and young men preparing for the ministry what they should read. Read the Bible. I would give the same answer five hundred times, over and above all other things, study the Bible.[1]

A young man in New York plied me with his questionings and debatings recently, but finally he settled down to his Bible and prayer, and God sanctified him and so filled and overwhelmed him with joy that he asked the Lord to stay His hand, for the blessings and glory were more than he could endure. And he wanted to wire me four hundred miles away to tell the story.

Familiarity with what the Bible says, with its doctrines and standards, will avail nothing unless the teaching of the Bible is translated into conduct, into character, into life. It is not enough to know or to approve this, but with our undivided will—our whole being—we must choose to be holy. Without the doctrine, the standard, the teaching, we shall never find the experience. Or, having found it, we shall be likely to lose it. Without the experience we shall neglect the teaching, we shall despise or doubt the doctrine, we shall lower the standard.

When Salvation Army officers (ministers) lose the experience, the holiness meetings (services) languish, and when the holiness meetings languish, the spiritual life of the corps (churches) droops and fails, and all manner of substitutes and expedients are introduced to cover up the ghastly facts of spiritual loss, disease, and death.

If we are to maintain our holiness standard, we must not only know the doctrine and experience in our own hearts, but we must teach it, preach it, and press it upon the people in season and out of season, until, like Paul, we can declare our faithfulness in "warning everyone and teaching everyone with all the wisdom God has given us. We want to present them to God, perfect in their relationship to Christ" (Col. 1:28 NLT).

Personally, I find that the surest way to get souls saved and restored—as well as the only way to get Christians sanctified—is to preach holiness plainly, constantly, and tenderly. Then not only do Christians see their need and privilege, but also sinners lose their self-complacency, discover their desperate condition, perceive the possibilities and joys of a true Christian life, and become inclined to surrender and be saved.

We shall greatly help ourselves and others if we carefully and constantly read and scatter holiness literature. There exists a library of books and papers on this subject that are plain, simple, scriptural, and full of the thrill, passion, and compelling power of life and experience. Let us scatter these books everywhere, but especially among our young people, urging them to read everything that has been published on the subject. Let us sow all lands deep with this literature, for then we shall surely reap a harvest of great richness and prepare the way for the generation which shall come after us.

If we would promote the experience of heart holiness each of us must judge him- or herself faithfully and soberly, but we must be generous and sympathetic in our judgment of others. We must help each other. Sharp, harsh criticism does not tend to promote holiness, and especially so when it is indulged in behind a person's back. Kindly, generous criticism which springs from love and from a desire to help, and which is preceded and followed by heart-searching and prayer that it may be offered and received in a true spirit and manner of brotherly love, will often work wonders in helping a soul. We must not cease testifying to the experience and preaching the doctrine and living the life simply because others fail. We must be faithful witnesses, and we shall someday prove that our labor has not been in vain. The Devil makes war upon this doctrine and experience. Let us resist him, and he will flee.

The world will mock or turn away. Let us overcome the world by our faith. Faithfulness to this truth and experience will sometimes require of us the endurance of hardness as good soldiers of Jesus Christ. Holy men and women do not live always in an ecstasy. Sometimes we pass through agony, and at such times the weakness of the flesh will test our firmness of purpose. But we must be true, and we shall "conquer though we die."[2]

I have known people who, when others have lapsed and failed, have remained clear in experience, definite in testimony, and true and generous in holy living, to become the saving salt and guiding light of their church. I have known pastors jubilant in this experience to leaven and bless a whole community.

We must not be faultfinding, neither must we whine and wail and dolefully lament "the good old days" which we may feel were better than these. But we must kneel down and pray in faith, and rise up and shout and shine and sing, and in the name of the Lord command the sun to stand still in the heavens till we have routed the Enemy and gotten the victory. "Thanks be to God, who always leads us as captives in Christ's triumphal procession and uses us to spread the aroma of the knowledge of him everywhere" (2 Cor. 2:14 NIV). "Not that we think we are qualified to do anything on our own. Our qualification comes from God. He has enabled us to be ministers of his new covenant.

This is a covenant not of written laws, but of the Spirit. The old written covenant ends in death; but under the new covenant, the Spirit gives life" (2 Cor. 3:5–6 NLT).

We must not forget that our sufficiency is of God—that God is interested in this work and waits to be our helper. We must not forget that with all our study and experience and knowledge and effort we shall fail unless—patiently, daily, hourly—we wait upon God in prayer and watchful faithfully for the help and inspiration of the Holy Spirit. It is He who opens our eyes and the eyes of our people to see spiritual things in their true relations. He melts the heart, bends the will, illuminates the mind, subdues pride, sweeps away fear, begets faith, and bestows the blessing. And He makes the testimony, the preaching, and the written word mightily effective.

A Salvation Army officer who had lost the blessing of holiness attended one of my officers' meetings and went away with her heart breaking after God. It was Thursday; she prayed nearly all that night. The next day she spent reading the Bible and *Helps to Holiness*, and crying to God for the blessing. Saturday she went about her duties but with a yearning cry in her heart for the blessing. Sunday morning came, and she was again wrestling with God, when suddenly the great deep of her soul was broken up and she was flooded with light and love and peace and joy. The Holy Spirit had come. She went to the meeting that morning and told her experience. The Spirit fell on her soldiers (members) and they flocked to the penitent form and sought and found. And His presence was an abiding presence with that officer. She went on in the power of the Spirit, from the command of little struggling corps, where she had barely held the work together, to larger and yet larger corps, where she had sweeping victory. If space allowed I could multiply such instances.

Our Lord still baptizes with the Holy Spirit and fire. He has given us a standard of holiness. He has given us a doctrine, and He wants to give us an experience that shall incarnate both standard and doctrine in a heavenly and all-conquering life.

A Chinese man got full salvation and his neighbors said, "There is no difference between him and the Book." That should be said of you and me.

"There is a river whose streams make glad the city of God" (Ps. 46:4 ESV). You and I live on the banks of that river. Let us bathe in its waters, and then we will be like the blessed one who trusts in the Lord, who is as a tree planted by the waters, spreading out its roots by the river, and thriving forevermore (see Jer. 17:7–8).

NOTES

1. Charles Grandison Finney, *Lectures to Professing Christians* (New York: John S. Taylor, 1837), 311.

2. Daniel O. Teasley, "Stand by the Cross," 1907, public domain.

The Terror of the Lord **10**

The majesty of God's law can be measured only by the terrors of His judgments. God is rich in mercy, but He is equally terrible in wrath. As high as His mercy is, so deep is His wrath. Mercy and wrath are set over against each other as are the high mountains and deep seas. They match each other as day and night, as winter and summer, right and left, or top and bottom. If we do not accept mercy, we shall surely be overtaken by wrath.

God's law cannot be broken with impunity. "The soul who sins shall die" (Ezek. 18:20 ESV). We can no more avoid the judgment of God's violated law than we can avoid casting a shadow when we stand in the light of the sun or avoid being burned if we thrust our hand in the fire. Judgment follows wrongdoing as night follows day.

This truth should be preached and declared continually and everywhere. It should not be preached harshly (as though we were glad of it) nor thoughtlessly (as though we had learned it as a parrot might learn it) nor lightly (as though it were really of no importance). But it should be preached soberly, earnestly, tearfully, and intelligently, as a solemn, certain, awful fact to be reckoned with in everything we think and say and do.

The terrible judgments of God against the Canaanites were but flashes of His wrath against their terrible sins. People with superfine sensibilities mock at what they consider the barbarous ferocity of God's commands against the inhabitants of Canaan, but let such people read the catalogue of the Canaanites' sins as recorded in Leviticus (see 18:6–25), and they will understand why God's anger waxed so hot. The Canaanites practiced the most shameless and inconceivable wickedness, until, as God said, "Even the land was defiled" (Lev. 18:25 NIV).

"Fools mock at sin," wrote Solomon (Prov. 14:9 NASB), and professedly wise men and women still lead simple souls astray as the serpent beguiled Eve, saying, "You will not surely die" (Gen. 3:4 ESV).

But those who understand the unchangeable holiness of God's character and law tremble and fear before Him at the thought of sin. They know that He is to be feared; "the terror of the Lord" (2 Cor. 5:11 KJV) is before them. And this is not inconsistent with the perfect love that casts out fear (see 1 John 4:18). Rather, it is inseparably joined with that love, and the person who is most fully possessed of that love is the one who fears most—with that reverential fear that leads him or her to depart from sin. For the one who is exalted to the greatest heights of divine love and fellowship in Jesus Christ sees most plainly the awful depths of the divine wrath against sin and the bottomless pit to which souls without Christ are hastening.

This vision and sense of the exceeding sinfulness of sin and of God's wrath against wickedness begets not a panicky, slavish fear that makes a person hide from God, as Adam and Eve hid among the trees of Eden, but a holy, filial fear that leads the soul to come out into the open and run to God to seek shelter in His arms and be washed in the blood of the "Lamb of God who takes away the sin of the world!" (John 1:29 NLT).

Lo! On a narrow neck of land,
'Twixt two unbounded seas I stand;
Yet how insensible!
A point of time, a moment's space,
Removes me to that heavenly place,
Or shuts me up in hell!

Before me place, in dread array,
The scenes of that tremendous day,
When Thou with clouds shalt come
To judge the people at Thy bar;
And tell me, Lord, shall I be there
To hear Thee say, "Well done!"

Be this my one great business here,
With holy joy and holy fear,
To make my calling sure;
Thine utmost counsel to fulfill,
To suffer all Thy righteous will,
And to the end endure.[1]

NOTE

1. Charles Wesley, "Thou God of Glorious Majesty," 1749, public domain.

Holy Covetousness 11

"Covet earnestly the best gifts," wrote Paul to the church at Corinth (1 Cor. 12:31 KJV). Not the highest promotions, not the best positions, but "the best gifts," those gifts God bestows upon the people who earnestly desire them and diligently seek Him.

Nero sat upon the throne of the world. He held the highest position imaginable. But a poor, despised Jew in a dungeon in Rome, whose head Nero cut off like a dog's head, possessed the best gifts. And while Nero's name rots, Paul's name and works are a foundation upon which the righteous build for centuries and millenniums.

There were deacons, archdeacons, and venerable bishops and archbishops in England, some hundreds of years ago, who held high places and power and to whom others bowed low. But a poor, despised tinker in the filthy Bedford jail had earnestly desired and received the best gifts. And while those church dignitaries are forgotten by most, the world knows and loves the saintly tinker, John Bunyan, and is ever being made better and lifted nearer to God by his wise works and words.

You and I should seek these best gifts with all our hearts, and we should be satisfied with nothing short of them. It makes little difference what our position and rank may be; if we have these gifts, we shall have a name and bless the world. But without them, we shall prove to be only sham—painted fire and hollow mockery—and the greater our position and the higher our rank, the greater shams we are, and the greater will be our shame in God's great day of reckoning.

What are these gifts?

There is one that in a sense includes them all—the gift of the Holy Spirit. Have you received the Holy Spirit? Is He dwelling in your heart? Covet Him. Live not a day without His blessed presence in you.

Then there is the gift of wisdom. Covet this. The world is full of foolish men and women who don't know how to save themselves, nor how to promote salvation and peace among their fellow foolish ones who miss the way, who stumble along in darkness and perish in their folly. The world needs wise men and women, people who know when to speak, what to say, and when to be silent—people who know God and His way and walk in it.

God gives wisdom to those who seek Him. "If you need wisdom, ask our generous God, and he will give it to you" (James 1:5 NLT). Nothing will so distinguish you and exalt you among your contemporaries as fullness of wisdom.

There are several marks by which to know this heavenly wisdom. James tells us what they are. He said in James 3:17 that the wisdom that comes from above is:

- "Pure." Those who are truly wise will keep themselves pure. They will flee from all impurity in thought, word, and act. Filthy habits of every kind are broken and put away by this heavenly wisdom.
- "Peace loving." Those who have this gift and wisdom from God do not meddle with strife. They seek peace and run after it (see 1 Pet. 3:11). They are essentially peacemakers. They have learned the secret of the "soft answer" (Prov. 15:1 NKJV) which turns away wrath. They are not quick to take offense.
- "Gentle." Those who live in the spirit of this world may be rough and boorish, but those who are wise from above are gentle and considerate. And this gentleness may exist in the same heart with lion-like strength and determination. Jesus was as a "Lamb slain" (Rev. 13:8 KJV), but He was also "the Lion of the tribe of Judah" (Rev. 5:5 KJV). He was gentle as a mother and at the same time immeasurably strong.
- "Willing to yield." Though they are sinned against seventy times seven in a day, yet those who are heavenly wise stand ready to forgive (see Matt. 18:21–35). Their hearts are exhaustless fountains of goodwill. While, if it be their lot to lead, they "take the responsibility seriously" (Rom. 12:8 NLT) and, if necessary, with vigor, yet they do not count their lives dear to themselves (see Acts 20:24) but are willing to lay down their lives for the good of others (see 1 John 3:16).

- "Full of mercy and the fruit of good deeds." Like their heavenly Father they are "rich in mercy" (Eph. 2:4 KJV).
- "No favoritism." They are not partisans. They rise above party and class prejudice and are lovers of all. They stand for "the fair deal."
- "Always sincere." There is no guile in their hearts, no white lies on their tongues, no double-dealing in their actions. They are square and open and above-board in all their ways and dealings. They live in constant readiness for the judgment day.

Thank God for such wisdom, which He waits to bestow upon all those who covet it and who ask for it in faith. Covet wisdom.

Then there is the gift of faith. Covet faith. In everyone there is, in some measure, the power to believe, but added to this is a gift of faith that God bestows upon those who diligently seek Him. Covet this! Be steady, strong, intelligent believers. Cultivate faith. Stir it up in your hearts as you stir up the fire in your stove. Feed your faith on God's Word.

I once heard a mighty evangelist say that he used to pray and pray for faith, but one day he read, "Faith cometh by hearing, and hearing by the word of God" (Rom. 10:17 KJV). Then he began to study God's Word and hide it in his heart, and his faith began to grow and grow until through faith his works girded the globe. Covet faith.

Again, there is the gift of the spirit of prayer. Everybody can pray, if they will, but how few have the spirit of prayer! How few make a business of prayer and wrestle with God for blessing and power and wisdom! Real prayer is something more than a form of words or a hasty address to God just after breakfast, before worship, or before going to bed at night. It is an intense, intelligent, persistent council with the Lord, in which we wait on Him, reason and argue and plead our cause, listen for His reply, and will not let Him go till He blesses us. But how few pray in this way! Let us covet earnestly and cultivate diligently the spirit of prayer.

We should also covet the spirit of prophecy—that is, the ability to speak to the hearts and minds of others so that they shall see and feel that God is in us and in our words (see 1 Cor. 14:1–3). We may not be able to preach like William Booth, but there is probably not one of us who cannot preach and prophesy far more pungently, powerfully, and persuasively than we do if we earnestly coveted this gift and sought it in fervent prayer, faithful study, and constant and deep meditation. God would help us, and how greatly it would add to our power and usefulness! Let us earnestly covet this gift, asking God to touch our lips with fire and grace. The people wondered at the gracious words of Jesus, so why should we not be such mouthpieces for Him that they shall wonder at our gracious words too!

Solomon said, "Whoever loves a pure heart and gracious speech will have the king as a friend" (Prov. 22:11 NLT). And Paul said, "Let your speech always be gracious" (Col. 4:6 ESV).

But, above all, covet a heart full and flaming and overflowing with love. Pray for love. Stir up what love you have. Exercise love. It is good to take the Bible and, with a concordance, hunt out the word *love* until you know all the Bible says on the subject. And then with a heart full of love, pour it out on the children, the wandering ones, cranky folks, and poor loveless souls, until that wondrous text has its fulfillment in you: "May those who love [God] rise like the sun in all

its power!" (Judg. 5:31 NLT). How the frost and snows melt, the frozen
earth thaws, the trees burst into bud and leaf, the flowers blossom, the
birds sing, and all nature wakes to a revelry of life and joy when the
sun rises in all its power!

And we may be so full of love and faith and power and the Holy
Spirit that we shall be like that. Then indeed we shall be a blessing.
Souls dead in trespasses and sin shall come to life under our loving ministry and message. The weak shall be made strong, the sorrowing shall
receive divine comfort, the ignorant shall be taught, and heavenly light
shall illumine those that are in darkness. Let us then "covet earnestly
the best gifts" (1 Cor. 12:31 KJV).

A Common yet Subtle Sin 12

There is a sin which a priest once declared that no one had ever confessed to him — a sin so deadly that the wrath of God comes upon men and women because of it; a sin so common that probably everybody has at some time been guilty of it; a sin so gross in God's sight as to be classed with sexual immorality, idolatry, murder, and such like; a sin so subtle that those most guilty of it seem to be the most unconscious of it. It is a sin that has led to the ruin of homes, the doom of cities, the downfall of kings, the overthrow of empires, the collapse of civilizations, and the damnation of an apostle of ministers of the gospel and of millions of less conspicuous souls. People in the highest and most sacred positions of trust and who enjoy the most unlimited confidence of others have, under the spell of this sin, wrecked their good names and have brought shame to their families, and misfortune, want, and woe to their associates.

When God gave the Ten Commandments to Moses amid the thunder and lightning of Mount Sinai, one of the ten was against this sin. When Lot lost all he had in the doom of Sodom and Gomorrah, it was primarily because of this sin. When Nadab and Abihu were suddenly consumed by the fierce fires of God's wrath, at the bottom of their transgression was this sin. When Achan and his household were stoned, it was because of this sin. When Eli and his sons lost the priesthood and died miserably, it was at root because of this sin. When Saul lost his kingdom, it was because this sin had subtly undermined his loyalty to God. When Ahab died and the dogs licked his blood, he was meeting the doom of this sin. When David fell from heights of God's tender favor and fellowship, brought shame and confusion upon himself, and incurred God's hot displeasure and lifelong trouble, it was because of this sin. When Elisha's servant, Gehazi, went out from the presence of the prophet smitten with leprosy white as snow, it was because of this sin. When Judas betrayed the Master with a kiss, thus making his name a synonym of everlasting obloquy, and bringing upon himself the death of a dog and a fool, it was because of this sin. When Ananias and Sapphira dropped dead at Peter's feet, they suffered the dread penalty of this sin. When World War I burst forth in 1914, enveloping the earth in its wrathful flame, sweeping away the splendid young manhood of the world in storms of steel and rivers of blood, and engulfing the accumulated wealth of ages in a bottomless pit of destruction, the disaster could be traced to the unrestricted and deadly workings of this awful, secret, silent, pitiless sin.

What is this sin that the priest never heard mentioned in his confessional, this sin that apostles and priests and shepherds and servants have committed, and upon which the swift, fierce lightning of God's wrath has fallen—this sin of which everyone at some time has probably been guilty and yet which is so secret and subtle that those most enthralled by it are most unconscious of it?

When the herdsmen of Lot and Abraham fell into strife, Abraham, the uncle, to whom God had promised all the land, said to the young man, Lot, his nephew, "Let there be no strife between you and me, and between your herdsmen and my herdsmen, for we are kinsmen" (Gen. 13:8 ESV). Then he invited Lot to take any portion of the land that pleased him, and he would be content to take what was left. Lot looked down upon the fertile plains of Jordan and without a thought for his old uncle, to whom he owed all, drove his herds into the lush pastures of the rich plain, near the markets of opulent Sodom and Gomorrah, while the rough and stony hill country was left to Abraham. But God became, more fully than ever, the companion and portion of Abraham, while Lot, through his covetousness, was soon so entangled in the life of Sodom that in the doom of the city he lost all he had, barely escaping with his life, and accompanied only by two weak and willful daughters.

At the bottom of Nadab and Abihu's sacrilegious offering of strange fire before the Lord was their coveting of Aaron's priestly power and authority, and it led to God's swift vindication of Aaron in their awful destruction. When the children of Israel entered the Land of Promise and the walls of Jericho fell before them, Achan saw gold and garments which he coveted and took for himself, regardless of God's commandment, thereby bringing defeat to Israel, death to his fellow soldiers, and terrible doom to himself.

Old Eli's sons, unsatisfied with the rich provision made for the priesthood, coveted that which God had reserved for sacrifice, and against protest took for themselves what was forbidden. They also—despite God's command—coveted the wives and maidens who came to worship at God's altar. When softhearted old Eli heard about their sin, he only feebly reproved them. Consequently, God's wrath swiftly followed, with its doom of death and the loss of the priesthood.

It was Saul's coveting the goodwill of the people rather than the favor of God that led to his disobedience and loss of the kingdom.

Among all Ahab's other reeking iniquities, it was his coveteousness—which led him to destroy Naboth and steal his vineyard—that brought down upon him God's sleepless judgment, till he died in battle and dogs licked up his blood.

David coveted Bathsheba—the wife of another man—and to this day blasphemers sneer and God is reproached, while David escaped the doom that falls on those who are guilty of this sin only by his humble confession, deep repentance, and brokenness of heart. But he could not escape endless shame, sorrow, and trouble.

Gehazi cast longing eyes upon the gold, silver, and rare garments which Naaman pressed upon Elisha the prophet out of gratitude for his cleansing in Jordan, and which Elisha had refused. But, blinded by the glitter of gold and steeped in covetousness, Gehazi had no heart and no understanding for the austere self-denial of the fine old prophet, and he said to himself, "I will chase after him and get something from him" (2 Kings 5:20 NLT). And so he did! Then, to hide his sin, he lied to Elisha. But the old seer's eyes were like seraph's eyes—they saw—and he said to the covetous, lying Gehazi, "'Don't you realize that I was there in spirit when Naaman stepped down from his chariot to meet you? Is this the time to receive money and clothing, olive groves and vineyards, sheep and cattle, and male and female servants? Because you have done this, you and your descendants will suffer from Naaman's leprosy forever.' When Gehazi left the room, he was covered with leprosy; his skin was white as snow" (2 Kings 5:26–27 NLT).

Covetousness ruled Judas's stony, ashen heart, and for thirty pieces of silver he betrayed the Master!

Covetousness possessed the selfish hearts of Ananias and Sapphira. They wanted the praise and honor of utmost sacrifice and generosity while secretly holding on to their gold. And God smote them dead!

As we study the history and biblical examples of this sin of covetousness, we see the deep meaning and truth of Paul's words to Timothy: "People who long to be rich fall into temptation and are trapped by many foolish and harmful desires that plunge them into ruin and destruction. For the love of money is the root of all kinds of evil" (1 Tim. 6:9–10 NLT).

This sin in Lot led to ingratitude toward his uncle and neighborly association with vile sinners. In Nadab and Abihu, it led to envy and jealousy and sacrilege. It led to disobedience in Saul, to sacrilege and licentiousness in Eli's sons, to adultery and murder in David, to brazen robbery in Ahab, to greed and lying in Gehazi, to the betrayal of the innocent Christ with an impudent kiss in Judas, and to bold lying to the Holy Spirit in Ananias and Sapphira. Truly, from its poisonous root has sprung up the deadly, poisonous tree of all evil, and upon it in manifold ways has been outpoured the wrath of God, showing His holy hatred and abhorrence of it.

A close study of the awful ravages of this sin in its workings would show that again and again it has undermined thrones and led to the downfall of empires, and that it has rotted away the strong foundations of chastity and honesty and truth and goodwill in whole peoples, ending in the collapse of civilizations.

Once its workings begin in a human heart there is no end to the ruin and woe it may bring about in that soul, and then in the lives of others. There is no height of honor and holiness from which it may not pull men and women down. There is no depth of pitiless selfishness, lying evasion, brazen effrontery, and self-deception into which it may not plunge them. When proclaiming the Ten Commandments from the flaming mount, God reserved the last to hurl at this sin, not because it was least of all the sins forbidden, but rather because it was a pregnant mother of them all, an instigator and ally of all evil.

Covetousness is a sin that reaches out for people of every age. In some of its forms, it makes its most successful assaults upon those who are well advanced in years. Those in ardent devotion to Christ may successfully resist it in their youth and yet fall before it when their heads are crowned with honors and white with the snows of many winters. The fear of want in old age, the natural desire to provide for children and loved ones, may silently, secretly lead them into the deadly embrace of this serpent-like sin and shipwreck their honor, their faith, their "first love," their simplicity in Christ, their unselfish devotion to the interests of the Lord and the souls of others. Thus it may bring about their final rejection in that day when the secrets of their hearts shall be revealed and their works made manifest by fire.

How may we avoid this deadly, secret, subtle sin? There is but one way—that is, by following Jesus in daily, resolute self-denial, by watchfulness and prayer, by walking in the light as He is in the light, by openness of heart and humility of mind, by utter surrender to the Holy Spirit, by counting all things loss for Christ, by learning and not forgetting that "godliness with contentment is great gain" (1 Tim. 6:6 KJV), by seeking first the kingdom of God and His righteousness, by joyfully trusting and obeying those words of Peter—"Give all your worries and cares to God, for he cares about you" (1 Pet. 5:7 NLT)—and by keeping the heart clean.

"Blessed are the pure in heart: for they shall see God," said Jesus (Matt. 5:8 KJV). "Take care, and be on your guard against all covetousness" (Luke 12:15 ESV).

Sins against Chastity 13

After the preceding chapter appeared as an article in various periodicals in other countries, I received a communication from across the sea, in which a man wrote, "I observe that you make a statement concerning Eli with which I do not altogether agree." The writer said he does not consider Eli's appeal to his sons to be weak, as I stated in the article. Then he compared the sins of the sons of Eli (see 1 Sam. 2:12–17, 22–25) with the sins of Samuel's sons (see 1 Sam. 8:1–3). He argued that the sins of Samuel's sons were more heinous than the sins of Eli's sons, "one of which," he wrote, "was a sin against morality, a natural following out of an instinct for the propagation of the race, and the other a violation of a ceremonial law. But the dealings of Samuel's sons constituted a violation of fundamental righteousness."

Then my correspondent questioned why such terrible judgments fell upon Eli and his sons, while—so far as the record shows—Samuel and his sons escaped. Finally, he asked, "Why this differentiation? Do you consider that it is a more heinous sin to go against forms and ceremonials in connection with religion than it is to deal unrighteously with your neighbor?"

This letter raises the question of the comparative wickedness of sins against womanhood and chastity—a question that is seldom discussed except in private or in scientific or semi-scientific books that are not widely read. If I may, I wish to reply to it publicly, as follows.

First, I have no lawyer's brief for Samuel. He is one of the very few men in the Bible of whom no ill thing is written. He seems to have been acceptable to God from his youth up, and since God has recorded no charge against him I can bring none. "It is before his own master that he stands or falls" (Rom. 14:4 ESV). I can only rejoice with him, as a brother, in his victorious life and walk with God. There is no record as to how Samuel dealt with his miscreant sons, but since he retained God's favor he must have acted in harmony with God's will. I have no doubt, however, that his sons were rewarded according to their works, if not in this world then in the next, even though no mention of it is made in the Bible.

As regards Eli, he seems to have been a kindly old man, but weak in his abhorrence and condemnation of evil, at least in his own sons. God tells us plainly His reasons for dealing as He did with the old man and his vicious sons: "Because his sons are blaspheming God and he hasn't disciplined them" (1 Sam. 3:13 NLT). He knew their evil. As judge and high priest, Eli had the authority and power to stop the evil doings of his sons. And, according to the law of the land (which was the law of God), it was his duty to do so; therefore Eli should have acted. But all he did was offer a feeble reproof. My correspondent objected to my description and wrote, "To me it seems one of the most pathetic and moving appeals that an aged father could make to reprobate sons; he points out to them in moving language the difference between sinning against man and sinning against God."

But Eli was not only a father—he was a ruler, clothed with authority and power. He should therefore have done more than make "a pathetic and moving" appeal. He should have exercised all the authority and power of his great office to put a stop to the vile practices of his reprobate sons. "Whoever loves father or mother more than me is not worthy of me," said Jesus (Matt. 10:37 ESV). "Cursed is he who does the work of the LORD with slackness" (Jer. 48:10 ESV).

Eli might have saved himself, and possibly his boys, if he had acted promptly and vigorously—as he should have—and as a righteous ruler abhorring evil and bent on protecting the sacred rights of society and the reverent worship of God. It is the duty of a ruler to rule diligently (see Rom. 12:8) and impartially, and of a priest to insist on reverence in the service of God. There Eli failed, so the terrible and swift judgment of God cut him and his family down, and the priesthood and judgeship passed to others.

As to the comparative heinousness of the sins of the two sets of men, the sin of Eli's sons was far the worse. Any right-minded individual who considers what it would mean to have the sacred shelter of home invaded and the purity of wife or sister or daughter assailed must admit this. To rob someone of money is bad, but to rob a woman of her virtue is worse. To defraud someone in a court of justice and mete out injustice is vile, but to rob someone of the sanctity of home and the purity of wife or mother or sister or daughter is far viler. To debauch the future mothers of the race, and so to rob unborn children and generations yet to be of the noblest of all rights—the right of pure, sweet, holy, reverent motherhood—seems to me like poisoning the wells and springs from which cities must drink or perish, and hence the darkest of all crimes.

All the moralities and sanctions of religion were despised and cast away, and all the sacred rights of humanity were trampled upon and imperiled by Eli's apostate sons. They were set apart as the heralds and guardians of both religion and morality, yet their actions seem to have been the grossest insult to both God and humankind, and the most flagrant neglect and violation possible of their high and sacred calling.

My correspondent wrote that the offense of Eli's sons was "a natural following out of the instinct for the propagation of the species," as though that were some relief of their crime. But among all nations, and even among savage races, there is a higher instinct that forbids people from following the lower instinct, except lawfully, and among many tribes the punishment was death where this law was violated. Further, it was not the propagation of the species but the gratification of lust that moved these sons of Eli, as it is with all who break the law of chastity. The propagation of the species is the last thing such people desire, the one thing they wish to avoid.

The instinct and power of reproduction is the noblest physical gift God has bestowed upon humanity. It makes us partners with God in the creation of the race, and therefore the prostitution of that noble instinct and power is the vilest and worst of all crimes. It has brought into the world more sorrow, shame, disease, ruin, and woe than probably all other crimes combined.

It is far more dangerous to the morals and ultimate well-being of society (to say nothing of the sin against God) for ministers of religion in exalted positions, such as were Eli's sons, to fall into open, flagrant, unblushing immorality and sacrilege than for a judge to cause justice to miscarry, wicked as that is. We will war against and condemn the unjust judge, but what can we do when the sanctions of religion are destroyed, when the holy fear of God is lost, and when all the foundations of morality are rotted away—when our fathers are slaves of lust and full of corruption, and when the mothers of the race, who are our first and best teachers of righteousness and reverence, have no virtue?[1] "If the foundations be destroyed, what can the righteous do?" asked the psalmist (Ps. 11:3 KJV). The sins of Eli's sons seem to me to be in the forefront of the worst sins and crimes mentioned in the Bible or committed among the human race.

My correspondent asked, "Do you consider that it is a more heinous sin to go against forms and ceremonies in connection with religion than it is to deal unrighteously with your neighbor?" I answer, no! But the sons of Eli were doing far more than going "against forms and ceremonies in connection with religion." They were violating the most sacred rights of their neighbors, as well as robbing God of that reverent service which He claimed and which was His due, and so were bringing the service and worship of God into contempt and undermining all morality at one and the same time.

In all this I am not forgetting nor condoning the wickedness of Samuel's sons, nor do I suspect for an instant that they escaped the due judgments of God. Why there is no record of Him dealing with them we do not know. We do know, however, that the Bible declares the principles of God's moral government, and we may rest assured that in every instance He acts in harmony with those principles, whether or not we have a record of it.

NOTE

1. Brengle was referring to women who voluntarily enter into sexual sin—not those who have been forcibly raped. He would agree that a rape victim has committed no sin to deserve this outrageous act of violence against her.

Whitened Harvest Fields 14

Before fields are ready to harvest, they must be plowed and sowed and tilled. When Jesus said to His disciples, "Lift up your eyes, and see that the fields are white for harvest" (John 4:35 ESV), He looked upon a land plowed by God's faithful judgments, sowed deep with the toils and sacrifices of prophets and teachers from Moses to John the Baptist, and watered with the tears and blood of those who had sealed their testimony with their lives.

When young Adoniram Judson went, as the first American missionary, to Burma (today's Myanmar), he found a land covered with age-long growths of superstition and ignorance. For years he plowed and sowed in hope. He struggled with difficulties of language and spiritual darkness.

After seven years, with as yet no converts, a friend wrote and asked him what the prospects were. He replied, "The prospects are as bright as the promises of God."[1] Already the fields had whitened unto harvest, and shortly after he had written to his friend he was reaping what he had sown—thirty thousand souls were won to Jesus and organized for service.

It is not often that someone sows in tears and reaps in joy as Judson did. The plowers and sowers often toil in hope, and yet must wait for the reapers, who enter the fields and gather in the harvests upon which they themselves have bestowed no labor.

At the present time the world seems to be one vast ripened or ripening harvest field, waiting for earnest and skilled reapers. For many centuries it has been plowed and harrowed by wars and commotions, famine and pestilence, storm and earthquake, and where the plowshare has not reached, the spade of disappointment and sorrow, of bereavement and death, has left no sod unturned. Everywhere the soil has been and is being prepared.

Think of the tears that have been shed for a lost world over the years! So many have wept fountains of tears as they looked at men and women rejecting Jesus! Those tears have fallen like rain. They are a part of the sowing. God remembers them all. He treasures them in His bottle (see Ps. 56:8). Has He not said, "Those who plant in tears will harvest with shouts of joy. They weep as they go to plant their seed, but they sing as they return with the harvest" (Ps. 126:5–6 NLT)?

These tears of faithful workers will not be forgotten by God, and we must not forget them, but reckon with them, for they enter into the preparation of the harvest fields of the world.

Think of the prayers that have been offered over the years—prayers for the salvation of the world, for loved ones, children, and wayward and stumbling souls. Think of the prayers for enemies, for the friends of God and all workers of righteousness, in the secret closet, at the family altar, in the public hall, on the street, in the saloon, in the village, in the bungalow, in the city, in the desert, in the wilderness, in the jungle, on shipboard, and on trains, from lonely little quarters and from dying beds! These prayers ascend to God as incense, and they shall surely return in blessing. He does not forget them, and we must not. They have their part in the preparation of the harvest fields.

Think of the testimonies that have been given—testimonies to the enslaving power of sin and the heartache and dissatisfaction surely following its wildest pleasures; testimonies to the arresting, quickening, convicting power of the Holy Spirit, and to the absolute certainty He produces of a life beyond the grave and of judgment to come. Remember all the testimonies to forgiveness of sins, to the witness of the Spirit, and to the comfort of the Holy Spirit; testimonies to the subtle, lurking, hateful presence and power of inbred sin, and of deliverance and cleansing from all its defilement; testimonies to the incoming of the Holy Spirit and to love made perfect. Recall the continual witness to answered prayers, to divine guidance in times of perplexity, to healing in sickness, to deliverance from temptation, to revelations in times of darkness and loneliness, to fresh infusions of strength and hope in seasons of weakness and distress, to secret girdings for the long march and fierce conflicts of life, to renewals of patience and faith in the midst of backslidings and desolations, and to provision of which the world knows nothing (see John 4:32; Rom. 14:17).

Do not let us forget the great host who have ever proclaimed the spiritual realities of a blessed presence going before as a pillar of cloud and fire to the end of the way, of bending skies, of opening heavens, of songs and shoutings, of playing harps, of waving palms, and of rushing angel wings. And last of all, testimonies in the valley to Jesus, the Good Shepherd, folding His dear ones in the eternal embrace of His infinite love, and to triumph forever over death and hell. Oh, the power of testimonies! They have their part in the preparation of the harvest fields.

Think of the songs of the church, including The Salvation Army! How they have captured and held the attention of the world! The careless sinner and the ripened saint alike are arrested by them. How they soften the heart, recall memories of innocent childhood and of mothers' prayers! How they make one see the infant Jesus in the manger, the wrestling Savior in the garden, the dying Son of God on the cross, the bursting tomb, and the great white throne! They interest, alarm, convict, convert, assure, comfort, correct, inspire, guide, instruct, and illumine. They present the law in its most solemn and searching aspects, they declare the judgments of God, they proclaim the gospel in its most tender and fullest invitations, and they embrace all the vital Bible truths. And think how they are sung from the cradle to the grave! Everywhere they are heard and known, and their sound has gone forth to the ends of the earth. They have reached the hearts of men. Songs have their part—an immense part—in the preparation of the harvest fields.

But when we consider the seed sown by Christian workers and Salvation Army soldiers and officers in the fields of the world, we must add to those tears and prayers and testimonies and songs the vast library of literature filled with burning messages of love, yearning appeals, faithful warnings, thrilling experiences, and patient instructions broadcast over the nations.

And to all this must be added the immeasurable influence of saintly lives in shops and mills, in offices and stores, in mines and kitchens, on battlefields and shipboard—the sacrifices, devotion, faithful, patient service, and loving ministries which may be unheralded, and yet which silently hasten the ripening of the harvest.

Truly, with such seed-sowing the harvest must be great, and already it is whitened and waiting for the reapers. Oh, that the Lord of the harvest may send forth reapers into the whitened fields!

When the harvest is ripe, it must be gathered in haste, or it will be lost forever.

Our harvest is at hand. The children are waiting for us to gather them into the Savior's fold. The great crowds of wandering souls at home and abroad need our faithful ministry speedily. How shall we reach them? Where shall we begin? What shall we do?

We must determine to reach them. There must be mighty ingatherings of the people. To this end there must be mighty outpourings of the Spirit, and for this we must give ourselves fully to God. "The one who reaps draws a wage," said Jesus (John 4:36 NIV). Would you like God for your paymaster?

Then we should give ourselves to Him and do His work. If we do this and wait in faith upon Him, we shall see such Pentecosts and revivals as shall pale all those that have gone before.

If we cannot go ourselves, we may send generous help, that others may be sent. Some time ago I met a plain, humble, little woman at one of our camp meetings (revivals) who supported a missionary in

a foreign field, was educating his boy, and at the same time was sup-
porting a poor, friendless, old man in her home city. She did it by bak-
ing and selling her pies and cake and bread, and putting the proceeds
into God's work. God will surely see that she receives wages.

A comparatively poor man in California, of whom a friend of mine
wrote, supports eight foreign missionaries. When asked how he did it,
he replied that he lived simply and economically. In other words, he
denied himself to help to save the world for whom Jesus died. God
will see that he receives wages.

Then we can send books and letters out into the fields to reap for
us. A gentleman of whom I heard smoked four cigars a day. He
learned that for the price of a cigar he could buy a New Testament, and
then and there he resolved to quit smoking and with the money saved
to buy and scatter New Testaments, which he has since done at the
rate of more than one thousand per year. Some time ago a gentleman
living hundreds of miles away was passing through this man's native
city. He got off the train and spent the day searching for him to thank
him for the salvation he had received through the gift of one of those
New Testaments. He, too, shall surely receive wages. A letter of cheer
and sympathy sent to a distant, lonely reaper in some faraway field
will often hearten the worker and hasten the ingathering of the harvest.

Finally, we can all aid in the reaping of the harvest by watchful diligence and expectant faith in prayer. Did not Jesus command us to pray to
the Lord of the harvest to send forth laborers? And shall we not fulfill so
simple and yet so urgent a command? Multitudes cannot go to fields of
active service; many have but little, if any, money to send; but all can
pray and plead His promises till He rains righteousness upon the earth.

I know a man intimately who offered himself for foreign service but was rejected. Then he sought and obtained the fullness of the Spirit and gave himself to prayer and such service as he could offer at home. God heard and answered his prayers and blessed his labors, and today he hears—from the four corners of the earth—of those who have been saved and sanctified and blessed through things he has said and done.

God will be well pleased with those who pray, will bless them, and will visit with grace the ends of the earth in answer to their petitions. And they shall surely receive wages.

O Lord, pour out the spirit of prayer upon Your people, and help us to win the world to You!

NOTE

1. David Shibley, *Great for God: Missionaries Who Changed the World* (Green Forest, AR: New Leaf Press, 2012), 49.

Encouraging One Another 15

Over and over again when Moses was preparing to give up his command to Joshua, he encouraged Joshua and exhorted him to "be strong and courageous" (Deut. 31:6, 7, 23 NLT). And so important was this matter, that when Moses was dead, God Himself spoke to Joshua and said, "Be strong and courageous." And again, "Be strong and very courageous." And a third time, "This is my command—be strong and courageous! Do not be afraid or discouraged. For the LORD your God is with you wherever you go" (Josh. 1:6, 7, 9 NLT).

Centuries after, we hear David chanting his glorious psalm and singing, "Wait patiently for the LORD. Be brave and courageous. Yes, wait patiently for the LORD" (Ps. 27:14 NLT).

Hundreds of years later we hear Jesus saying to His little flock, confronted by a proud, fierce religious hierarchy and a world weltering in sin and darkness, "Fear not, little flock" (Luke 12:32 KJV), and "Take courage" (Matt. 14:27 NLT).

Later still we find Paul, in prison waiting to face the monstrous Nero, writing to Timothy from Rome, and saying, "My son, be strong in the grace that is in Christ Jesus" (2 Tim. 2:1 KJV). And to the Ephesians he wrote, "Be strong in the Lord, and in the power of his might" (Eph. 6:10 KJV).

We get a most impressive lesson from the story of the twelve spies sent by Moses to spy out the land of Canaan. Caleb and Joshua returned with cheery hearts, full of courage, and exhorted the people to go up at once and take the land. But ten of the spies gave an evil report, and the people said, "Our brothers have made our hearts melt" (Deut. 1:28 ESV). So they, disheartened and afraid, turned back into the wilderness and wandered to and fro for forty years, till all of them perished there except Joshua and Caleb and the children who were not responsible for the unbelief and disobedience of the multitude.

Thus we learn from the example of our Lord, of Moses, of David, and of Paul, and from the bad effect of the spies' gloomy report, the importance of encouraging rather than discouraging one another. How shall we do this?

1. By keeping in such close touch and communion with God that our faces shine with inward peace and that the joy in our hearts bubbles out in hearty, happy, helpful testimony, not only in worship gatherings, but wherever we meet a brother or sister.

2. By talking more about our victories than our defeats, by thinking and meditating more upon our triumphs than our trials; by counting our blessings, naming them one by one; and by praising God for

what He has done and what He has promised to do. We should not ignore the dark side of things, but we should not magnify it and refuse to see the silver lining to the cloud that is so dark. God is neither dead nor dying, and He does not forget His people who cry to Him night and day, who wait upon Him and do His will. He can open the Red Sea for His people and drown their enemies in its floods (see Ex. 14). He can make Jericho's walls tumble down before His people who go faithfully about their work and who shout when the time comes (see Josh. 6). He can make the valley of dry bones teem with an army of living men (see Ezek. 37:1–14). Oh, He is a wonderful God, and He is our God! There is nothing too hard for Him (see Jer. 32:17). Therefore, we should trust Him, and encourage others to trust Him and to make their prayer to Him in faith and without ceasing.

3. By dwelling more upon the good than the bad in other people. If we would encourage each other, we should talk more about our brothers and sisters who are always exemplary, generous, hardworking, and faithfully serving than about those who are unfaithful, self-centered, and frivolous. We should think and talk more about leaders who by much prayer and work and diligence are bringing souls into the kingdom of God than about those who are embittered and faltering in their commitment.

4. By trying to comprehend something of the vast responsibilities and burdens that press upon our leaders. What a multitude of perplexities harass their minds and try their patience! Therefore we should not be too quick to criticize but more ready to pray for them and give them credit for being sincere and doing the best they can under the circumstances—probably as well or better than we ourselves

would do if we were in their place. They are helped by encouragement even as we are.

I know a Salvation Army officer who received his target for a special fund-raising effort and, without praying over it or looking to the Lord at all, immediately sat down and wrote to his superior a sharp letter of protest and complaint which discouraged him and made it much harder for him to go happily about his work. I know another old officer in that same area who got his target, which seemed fairly large. He saw his superior, and said, "I think you ought to do me a favor." The poor man's heart began to get heavy but at last he asked, "Well, what is it?" To his amazement and joy, the dear officer replied, "Major, I love The Salvation Army and its work, and I think you ought to increase my target." He encouraged his burdened brother, the major. He is an old officer who goes from one average corps to another, but through all the years and amid all the changes and trials and difficulties, he has kept cheery and trustful and sweet in his soul, and God makes him a blessing.

"They help each other and say to their companions, 'Be strong!'" (Isa. 41:6 NIV). Shall you and I not take that text for a motto? We shall save ourselves as well as others from discouragement if we do.

The influence of one gloomy soul can throw a shadow over a whole family. One person in a church who persistently represents the difficulties of every undertaking can slow down the pace of all. At best, they go forward burdened with that person's weight rather than quickened by his or her example. The glorious work of encouraging others is within the capacity of all. The weakest of us can at least say with loving zeal and earnest testimony, "Come, let us tell of the

LORD's greatness; let us exalt his name together. . . . Taste and see that
the LORD is good. Oh, the joys of those who take refuge in him!" (Ps.
34:3, 8 NLT).

Always he was the dullard, always he
Failed of the quick grasp and the flaming word
That still he longed for. Always other men
Outran him for the prize, till in him stirred
Black presage of defeat, and blacker doubts
Of love and wisdom regnant; and he styled
Himself disciple of the obvious,
Predestined failure, blundering fool and smiled.

But with the smile went heartbreak. Then one day
A little lad crept wailing to his knee,
Clasping a broken toy. "I slipped and fell
And broke it. Make another one for me."
Whereat the answer: "I am but a fool.
I can make nothing." "You can mend it then."
"At least I'll try." And patiently and slow
He wrought until the toy was whole again.

And so he learned his lesson. In the world,
The bustling world that has no time to spare
For its hurt children, all compassionate
He sought, and seeking found them everywhere.
And here he wove again a shattered dream,

And there bound up a bruised and broken soul;
And comrades of the fallen and the faint,
He steadied wavering feet to reach their goal.

Forgotten were his dreams of self and fame;
Forever gone the bitterness of loss;
Nor counted he his futile struggles vain,
Since they had taught him how to share the cross
Of weaker brother wisely; and henceforth
He knew no word but *service*. In it lay
Ambition, work, and guerdon, and he poured
His whole soul in the striving of the day.

And when at last he rested, as Love led,
So now it crowned him. And they came with tears—
Those sorrowing hearts that he had comforted—
Bearing the garnered triumphs of their years:
"Not ours, but His, the glory. Dreams come true,
Temptations conquered, lives made clean again,
All these and we ourselves are work of Him
Whom God had set the task of mending men."[1]

NOTE

1. Eleanor Duncan Wood, "A Mender of Men," *The Altoona Tribune*, May 5, 1913, 8.

How a Nobody Became a Somebody 16

It is one of the shortest, simplest stories ever heard, and yet one of the sweetest and most wonderful, as told by Luke. Jesus had been across the little sea and had cast out a legion of devils from a poor fellow. The devils, by His permission, went into a big herd of swine, and the swine rushed off down a precipice and drowned themselves in the sea. They preferred death to devils. Wise pigs!

The men who fed the pigs fled to the city and told what had been done. Then the people came out to Jesus and found the man out of whom the devils had been cast "sitting at Jesus' feet, fully clothed and perfectly sane." But—and this seems strange—"they were all afraid" (Luke 8:35 NLT). Then the people poured in from all the country and "begged Jesus to go away and leave them alone, for a great wave of fear swept over them" (Luke 8:37 NLT).

Jesus did not insist on His right to stay among them, but gently and quietly withdrew, leaving the newly delivered man to evangelize all that country. When Jesus returned to His own side of the sea, He found the people all waiting for Him, and they "welcomed [Him]" (Luke 8:40 NLT).

In the crowd was the ruler of the synagogue, Jairus, who "fell at Jesus' feet, pleading with him to come home with him. His only daughter, who was about twelve years old, was dying" (Luke 8:41–42 NLT). Jesus went, but as He went, "he was surrounded by the crowds" (Luke 8:42 NLT). It was a crowd bursting with curiosity, wondering what He would do next, and determined not to miss the sight. Jairus was an important person, and that added to the interest.

But in the town was a poor, pale-faced, hollow-cheeked, ill-clad woman, who had been sick with an issue of blood for twelve years. The people, no doubt, had grown very tired of seeing her shambling along week after week to see the doctors, upon whom she had spent all her living in a vain twelve years' search and struggle for health. She was just a "nobody"—everybody was tired of the sight of her— but into the throng she came with her bloodless face and tired eyes and shuffling feet and threadbare, faded clothes. The crowd jostled her, crushed her, trampled upon her feet, and blocked her way, but she had a purpose. She was inspired by a new hope. If she could only reach Jesus and touch the hem of His garment, she was sure her long struggle for health would be ended. And so, dodging, ducking under arms, edging her way through the jam of the great, moving crowd, she at last got close to Him, and, stretching forth a wasted, bony hand, she touched His travel-stained, rough, workman's robe, and something happened! Instantly a thrill of health shot through her, and she was well!

And something happened to Jesus! The crowd had been pressing upon and jostling Him, but He felt that touch and said, "Who touched me?" They all denied, and Peter spoke up, pointing out that many had touched Him. But one timid touch was different from all the rest. Jesus said, "Someone deliberately touched me, for I felt healing power go out from me" (Luke 8:46 NLT).

The nobody had suddenly become "somebody." And somebody she was in very truth from that day forth. "When the woman realized that she could not stay hidden, she began to tremble and fell to her knees in front of him. The whole crowd heard her explain why she had touched him and that she had been immediately healed" (Luke 8:47 NLT).

All eyes were turned upon her now. Jairus, the important ruler, was just one of the crowd. Other people were all "nobodies." No one in all that throng had eyes for anybody else but that shrinking, trembling woman, and Jesus.

And then the sweetest words she ever heard dropped from His dear lips: "'Daughter,' he said to her, 'your faith has made you well. Go in peace'" (Luke 8:48 NLT). And in peace she went.

I venture to think that from that hour she was by far the most interesting woman in that town. The people would talk about her. They would seek her out, and when she walked the street the children would stop their playing, the women their work, and the men their business, to look at her and watch her as far as their eyes could follow her.

She was now "somebody," eclipsing everybody else in that old town. No, not everybody! There was a twelve-year-old girl who was

most interesting and much talked about, too—Jairus's daughter. Jesus
was on the way to heal her when this woman stopped the procession,
and during the delay the little girl died.

Someone came and told Jairus, saying, "Your daughter is dead.
There's no use troubling the Teacher now" (Luke 8:49 NLT). But when
Jesus heard it, He answered, "Don't be afraid. Just have faith, and she
will be healed" (Luke 8:50 NLT). And He went and raised her from
the dead.

Now I am sure that while that woman was the most talked about
and most interesting woman in the town, that girl was the most interesting child. Those were the two "somebodies" of that whole country
round about, and the secret was that they had come into touch with
Jesus. Real faith in Jesus, vital union with Him, will always make an
interesting somebody out of a dull nobody.

The child couldn't go to Jesus; she was dead. So He went to her.
But the woman had to go to Jesus, and this was not easy. The crowd
was in the way, and possibly some of them purposely blocked her
way. Others may have sneered at her and asked her what was her
haste, and what she meant by edging in front of folks who had as
much right on the street as she. But she shut her ears, or heard as one
who was deaf. She kept her own secrets and pressed on as well as she
could until she touched Him. And that touch gave her all her heart's
desire and rewarded all her effort.

So, today, people who go to Jesus do not always find it easy. Other
people get in the way. Sometimes they stoutly oppose; sometimes they
sneer and ridicule. Cares and fears and doubts throng and press around
the seeker; darkness of mind and soul obscures the way. But there is

nothing else to do except to press on, right on and on. And those who press on and on will find Him, reach Him, touch Him, and get all their hearts' desires and be rewarded above all they ask or think.

It is true! I know it is, for I myself so sought and found Him and was satisfied. And He satisfies me still. He is a wonderful Savior!

Don't underestimate the power of God in you, nor yet what you, by working quietly and steadily with Him, may accomplish. Paul told us not to think too highly of ourselves (see Rom. 12:3). But he said of himself, "I can do all things through him who strengthens me" (Phil. 4:13 ESV). He thought of himself linked to the illimitable strength of Christ, and therefore omnipotent for any work Christ set him to do.

The future before you is big with opportunities and possibilities. Open doors on every hand invite you to enter and do service for the Master and for others, and the strength that worked in Paul works in you, if you do not hinder it by selfishness and unbelief.

No one can tell how much the future spread of God's kingdom may depend on you. "See how great a forest a little fire kindles!" (James 3:5 NKJV). Keep the fire of love and faith and sweet hopefulness burning in your heart, and you may start a blaze that will someday sweep the country or the world. Whoever you are—whether you are a respected leader or the newest follower of Jesus on earth—upon you the glory of the Lord may so shine that through you a great quickening may come to your corps, church, workplace, neighborhood, or home that will make the future so bright that the past will pale before it.

Would you like to be that man or woman? Then seek the Lord, daily, constantly, with your whole heart. Seek Him through His Word. Seek Him in secret prayer in the night watches and in the noonday. Seek Him in glad obedience. Seek Him in childlike faith. Seek nothing for yourself. "Do you seek great things for yourself? Seek them not" (Jer. 45:5 ESV) is the word of the Lord to you if you want Him to work mightily in you.

If honor comes, thank God, lay it at the torn feet of Jesus, and forget it, lest it ruin you. "Love . . . is not puffed up" (1 Cor. 13:4 NKJV). If honor comes not—if you seem to be forgotten in the distributions of rewards and honors and promotions—still thank God and go on. Seek the honor which comes from God alone, the honor of walking in the footsteps of Jesus, of loving, serving, sacrificing, suffering for others, and you shall have your reward. You surely shall, and it will be great, exceeding abundantly above all you ask or think. The crowning joy is yet to come. The final and all-sufficient and unfading rewards will be given by the Master's own hand. Don't worry if some lesser reward eludes you, lest through your fretting you lose the honor that comes from God alone and miss the crown Christ keeps in store for you. Beware of fretting over rewards and promotions and honors given by mere mortals! It is a snare set for you by the Enemy of your soul. Take your eyes off other people and see Jesus only. If others are good and spiritual and devoted to the Lord, emulate them, follow them as they follow Christ; but if they are faulty, don't worry about them (see Ps. 37:1–5), but pray for them and remember the word of Jesus to Peter: "What is that to you? You follow me!" (John 21:22 ESV).

Be filled with the spirit of Jonathan and his armor bearer. They went up alone and routed the Philistines. They were jealous for the glory of God and the overthrow of His impudent and insolent foes and were willing to jeopardize their lives to defeat God's enemies (see 1 Sam. 14).

Be filled with the spirit of Paul, who wrote, "Whatever gain I had, I counted as loss for the sake of Christ" (Phil. 3:7 ESV) and, "My life is worth nothing to me" (Acts 20:24 NLT) and, "I will very gladly spend and be spent for you; though the more abundantly I love you, the less I be loved" (2 Cor. 12:15 KJV).

May this spirit of Paul abound in you! This is holiness. This is heaven begun. This is the Spirit of Jesus still abiding in men and women.

Don't forget that "you He made alive, who were dead in trespasses and sins" (Eph. 2:1 NKJV). And don't forget "that few of you were wise in the world's eyes or powerful or wealthy when God called you. Instead"—note well—"God chose things the world considers foolish in order to shame those who think they are wise. And he chose things that are powerless to shame those who are powerful. God chose [What a chooser is God!] things despised by the world, things counted as nothing at all, and used them to bring to nothing what the world considers important. As a result, no one can ever boast in the presence of God. [But] God has united you with Christ Jesus" (1 Cor. 1:26–30 NLT).

My Testimony 18

Today (June 1, 1919), I am fifty-nine years old, and there is not a cloud in my spiritual heaven. My mouth is full of laughter and my heart is full of joy. I feel so sorry for folks who don't like to grow old, who are trying all the time to hide the fact that they are growing old and who are ashamed to tell how old they are. I revel in my years. They enrich me. If God should say to me, "I will let you begin over again, and you may have your youth back once more," I would say, "O dear Lord, if you do not mind, I prefer to go on growing old!"

I would not exchange the peace of mind, the abiding rest of soul, the measure of wisdom I have gained from the sweet and bitter and perplexing experiences of life, and the confirmed faith I now have in the moral order of the universe and in the unfailing mercies and love of God, for all the bright but uncertain hopes and tumultuous joys of youth. Indeed, I would not!

These are the best years of my life—the sweetest, the freest from anxious care and fear. The way grows brighter, the birds sing sweeter, the winds blow softer, the sun shines more radiantly than ever before. I suppose my outward man is perishing, but my inward man is being joyously renewed day by day.

Victor Hugo supposedly said, "For half a century I have been writing my thoughts in prose, verse, history, philosophy, drama, romance, tradition, satire, ode, songs. I have tried all. But I feel that I have not said the thousandth part of what is in me." And he said, "Winter is on my head [but] eternal spring is in my heart."[1] Truly, that is the way I feel these days.

One of the prayers of my heart as I grow older is that of David: "Now that I am old and gray, do not abandon me, O God. Let me proclaim your power to this new generation, your mighty miracles to all who come after me" (Ps. 71:18 NLT).

David was jealous for the glory of God and for the highest well-being of his own generation and every generation that was to follow. And he prayed no selfish prayer, but poured out his heart to God that he might so live and speak and write that God's glory and goodness and power might be made known to the people of his own time and to all who should come after him. And how wonderfully God heard and answered his prayer! Oh, that God would grant me a like grace!

If the eye of any friend falls upon this testimony, let me beseech you to unite with me and for me in this prayer of David, which I make my own.

This past year has been wonderful. Since the first of January, considerably over three thousand souls have knelt at the penitent form in my meetings, seeking pardon and purity. Seldom have I seen such manifestations of God's presence and power as during these months. I rejoice in God my Savior, and my soul magnifies the Lord (see Luke 1:46–47).

I wish I knew more of the secret of growing old gladly and could better tell it to others. But some lessons that I have learned, or partially learned, I here pass on: Have faith in God—in His providence, His superintending care, and His unfailing love. Accept the bitter with the sweet and rejoice in both. The bitter may be better for us than the sweet. Don't grow impatient and fretful. If you fall into many trials, count it all joy, knowing that the trial of your faith produces patience; "let patience have her perfect work, that you may be perfect and entire, wanting nothing" (James 1:4 KJV).

What a high state of grace that is—to be "perfect and entire, wanting nothing"! And yet it is to be attained through the joyful acceptance of annoying trials and petty vexations, as a part of God's discipline (see James 1:2–7).

Keep a heart full of love toward everybody. Learn to be patient with folks who try your patience. If you can't love them naturally and easily, then love them with compassion and pity. But love them, pray for them, and don't carry around hard thoughts and feelings toward them.

Here is a tender little poem by Whittier, our Quaker poet:

> My heart was heavy, for its trust had been
> Abused, its kindness answered with foul wrong;
> So, turning gloomily from my fellow men,
> One summer Sabbath day I strolled among
> The green mounds of the village burial place,

Where, pondering how all human love and hate
Find one sad level; and how, soon or late,
Wronged and wrong-doer, each with meekened face,
And cold hands folded over a still heart,
Pass the green threshold of our common grave,
Whither all footsteps tend, whence none depart,
Awed for myself and pitying my race,
Our common sorrow, like a mighty wave,
Swept all my pride away, and, trembling I forgave![2]

Don't waste time and fritter away faith by living in the past, by mourning over the failures of yesterday and the long ago. Commit them to God and look upward and onward. "Forgetting those things which are behind," said Paul, "and reaching forth unto those things which are before, I press toward the mark for the prize of the high calling of God in Christ Jesus" (Phil. 3:13–14 KJV).

Someone has said that there are two things we should never worry over and two days about which we should never be anxious. First, we should not worry over the things that we can help, but set to work diligently to help them. Second, we should not worry over the things that we cannot help, but commit them to God and go on with the duties close at hand. Again, we should not be anxious about yesterday; our anxieties will not mend its failures nor restore its losses. Second, we should not be anxious about tomorrow. We cannot borrow its grace. Why, then, should we borrow its care?

Give good heed to failing bodily strength. The Salvation Army's founder, William Booth, once said that the body and soul, being very near neighbors, have a great influence upon each other. We must remember that our bodies are to be treated like our beast, and Solomon said, "Whoever is righteous has regard for the life of his beast" (Prov. 12:10 ESV). When we were young, we could stay up all night, eat ice cream, nuts, and cake at midnight, and go about our work the next day, not much the worse, so far as we could judge, for the shameful mistreatment of our bodies. But woe unto men and women who, growing old, think they can treat their bodies so!

We must remember that our bodies are the temple of the Holy Spirit. Hence, while they need sufficient nourishing food and restful sleep, they must in no sense be pampered, and all nervous excesses must be strictly avoided or the body will react upon the mind and the spirit and weakness and impatience and gloom will cloud the soul. And then, instead of ripening into mellow sweetness with age, the soul will turn bitter and sour—and what can be more pitiful than an embittered and soured old soul?

But oh, the joy of living a life of sobriety, faith, quietness and confidence, of meekness, service, and love, and of "growing in every way more and more like Christ, who is the head of his body, the church" (Eph. 4:15 NLT). Such a life is never old, but eternally renewing itself, eternally youthful, like a springing, sparkling fountain that is fed by unfailing waters that flow down from the heights of the everlasting hills. "I take refuge in you, LORD. . . . How great is the goodness that you've reserved for those who honor you, that you commit to those who take refuge in you—in the sight of everyone!" (Ps. 31:1, 19 CEB).

Grow old along with me!

The best is yet to be,

The last of life, for which the first was made:

Our times are in His hand

Who saith, "A whole I planned,

Youth shows but half; trust God: see all, nor be afraid" . . .

Then, welcome each rebuff

That turns earth's smoothness rough,

Each sting that bids nor sit nor stand but go!

Be our joys three-parts pain!

Strive, and hold cheap the strain;

Learn, nor account the pang; dare, never grudge the throe! . . .

He fixed thee mid this dance

Of plastic circumstance,

This present, thou, forsooth, wouldst fain arrest;

Machinery just meant

To give thy soul its bent,

Try thee and turn thee forth, sufficiently impressed . . .

The future I may face now I have proved the past.[3]

NOTES

1. M. Houssaye, "When Victor Hugo Is a Hundred Years Old," *The Pennsylvania School Journal* 60, no. 2 (August 1911): 63–64. The text is from an imagined conversation between Hugo and four atheists.

2. John Greenleaf Whittier, "My Heart Was Heavy," eds. Eliakim Littell and Robert S. Littell, *Littell's Living Age* 129, no. 1662 (April 15, 1876): 130.

3. Robert Browning, "Rabbi Ben Ezra," *Poems of Robert Browning* (London: Oxford University Press, 1923), 636–638.

Samuel L. Brengle's Holy Life Series

This series comprises the complete works of Samuel L. Brengle, combining all nine of his original books into six volumes, penned by one of the great minds on holiness. Each volume has been lovingly edited for modern readership by popular author (and long-time Brengle devotee) Bob Hostetler. Brengle's authentic voice remains strong, now able to more relevantly engage today's disciples of holiness. These books are must-haves for all who would seriously pursue and understand the depths of holiness in the tradition of John Wesley.

Helps to Holiness
ISBN: 978-1-63257-064-2
eBook: 978-1-63257-065-9

The Heart of Holiness
ISBN: 978-1-63257-066-6
eBook: 978-1-63257-067-3

The Servant's Heart
ISBN: 978-1-63257-068-0
eBook: 978-1-63257-069-7

Ancient Prophets and Modern Problems
ISBN: 978-1-63257-070-3
eBook: 978-1-63257-071-0

Come Holy Guest
ISBN: 978-1-63257-072-7
eBook: 978-1-63257-073-4

Resurrection Life and Power
ISBN: 978-1-63257-074-1
eBook: 978-1-63257-075-8

Samuel L. Brengle's Holy Life Series Box Set
ISBN: 978-1-63257-076-5